Eating
CAN BE
Good
FOR YOU

Published for Presto,
Argyll House,
Millington Road, Hayes,
Middlesex UB3 4AY by
The KMS Partnership Ltd,
Mountbatten House,
Victoria Street,
Windsor, Berkshire SL4 1HE

Acknowledgements

Art directed and designed by
N/K Partnership

Home Economists
Roz Denny Judith Wiltshire

Photographer
Eric Carter

Stylist
Dawn Lane

Accessories
David Mellor, Sloane Street

Copy Editor
Cherry Lewis

Typesetter
Midford Typesetting Ltd

Printed and bound in Spain by
Printer Industria Gráfica SA, Barcelona
D.L.B. 31183-1985

ISBN O 948620 00 5

CONTENTS

Pork tenderloin stuffed with prunes p52; stir-fry summer medley p64; boiled potatoes; iced raspberry yogurt p76.

FOREWORD

There are lots of gloomy stories about the damage food is doing to health. The fact is, EATING CAN BE GOOD FOR YOU, but many men, women and children would be healthier and enjoy life more if they ate differently. Despite the vast amount of information about food and health the majority of people still think it's all aimed at 'someone else'. There is also a feeling that a healthier diet may not go down too well with the family. And even if you decide to eat less fat and more fibre, what do you actually eat for supper?

This book aims to translate all the advice about fats and fibre into food. Delicious food. It also aims to give you enough guidance so you'll know what to eat for supper and what to put on the shopping list. It contains over 100 recipes to help you give the family food they'll love. Whether you're a skilled cook or just learning, you'll enjoy making these dishes. You won't have to spend hours to achieve results that look as good as the photographs — nearly all the recipes can be prepared in less than 30 minutes.

Much of the advice given today about food and health suggests that snacks and informal meals can't be healthy. That is nonsense. But it may be one of the reasons why some people, who don't eat family meals three times a day, won't come to terms with eating differently. So, if you live in a household where formal meals are things of the past, this book is for you. There are dozens of ideas for healthy snacks. What's more, many of the recipes are so easy children can make them.

There are lots of family meals too, and some special dishes for entertaining — healthily of course!

If you need to lose weight, you'll find advice in the introduction on how to go about it. Every recipe is calorie-counted, too.

If you just want to make a few changes in your diet in order to eat less fat and more fibre, again the introduction and recipes will help. Equally, if you want to take the business of eating more seriously, you'll find all the information you need here.

This book answers questions about food and health as thoroughly as current knowledge will allow. In recent years a great deal has been learned about the affect of food on health but there are still questions that remain unanswered. However, enough is known to enable experts to recommend that we eat less fat and more fibre and that everyone should be the right weight.

EATING CAN BE GOOD FOR YOU aims to help you and your family achieve these objectives while still continuing to enjoy what you eat.

DOES IT MATTER WHAT WE EAT?

Everyone cares what food tastes like, but there's more to it than just selecting foods that taste good. The nutrients food supplies have a profound affect on health. Eating the right diet makes it easier to slim and stay slim, reduces the risk of having a heart attack and high blood pressure and improves dental health. Good food also means you'll have more vitality and enthusiasm for life. There's so much talk about fats and fibre it's easy to forget that food has to supply proteins, thirteen vitamins and dozens of minerals. *Some* fat is essential too.

These facts may make you wonder how anyone can choose foods wisely. In fact, it isn't too difficult. Very few people in Britain are short of vitamins or minerals, although many don't eat enough fibre. The problems are mainly to do with eating too much of certain foods.

The table explains briefly what some nutrients do and shows the main foods in which they occur. Those with * are the ones which need attention; many people are not eating the correct amounts to promote optimum health.

NUTRIENT	FUNCTION	MAIN FOOD SOURCES
PROTEINS	Form part of the structure of every cell in the body. Provide energy. Enzymes and some hormones are proteins	Lean meat, bread, fish, eggs, potatoes, pasta, flour, peas and other pulse vegetables
STARCHES	Provide energy	Bread, potatoes, rice, flour, breakfast cereals
SUGARS	Provide energy	Table sugar (sucrose), sweets, chocolate, cakes, sweet biscuits, honey, jam, many fruits
DIETARY FIBRE*	Helps food move through the intestine quickly. Prevents constipation	Wholemeal bread, peas, baked and haricot beans, bran-containing breakfast cereals, spinach, chick peas, red kidney beans, sweetcorn, blackberries, raspberries, fresh and dried currants, raisins, sultanas, figs, prunes
FATS		
Saturated*	Provide energy. Tend to increase blood cholesterol levels	Meat fat, butter, full-fat milk, hard margarine, cheese, palm and coconut oils, hydrogenated vegetable oils
Monounsaturated	Provide energy. No affect on blood cholesterol levels	Olive oil, poultry fat
Polyunsaturated	Provide energy and form part of the structure of every body cell. Also help form prostaglandins — essential for body function. Tend to lower blood cholesterol	Corn, sunflower, cotton seed and soya bean oils, herring, mackerel, polyunsaturated margarine
VITAMINS		
A — retinol	Keeps skin and lining of digestive system healthy. Helps vision in dim light	Cod-liver oil, liver, kidney, butter, margarine, carrots, spinach, milk, eggs, salmon, mackerel, herring
B Group B$_1$ — thiamin B$_2$ — riboflavin Nicotinic acid Pantothenic acid	Enable the energy in proteins, fats, starches, sugars and alcohol to be used. Allow nervous system to function	Wide range of meats, vegetables, fruits, cereal foods
Folic acid B$_{12}$	Help formation of healthy red blood cells	Folic acid — dark green vegetables, liver. B$_{12}$ — liver, kidney, eggs
Biotin	Aids fat metabolism	Liver, kidney, eggs, most other foods
B$_6$ — pyridoxine	Aids protein metabolism	Many meats, wholegrain cereals
C — ascorbic acid	Helps cement cells together, promotes wound healing	Orange, grapefruit, spinach, Brussels sprouts, cauliflower, blackcurrants, potatoes, strawberries. Many other fruits and vegetables contain some
D	Facilitates calcium absorption and deposition in bones. Keeps blood calcium and phosphorus levels stable	Cod-liver oil, margarine, kippers, herring. However, most is made in the body by the action of sunlight on skin
E	Not known in detail. Probably more important if food contains high levels of polyunsaturated fats	Vegetable oils, many cereal foods, eggs. Many other foods contain some
K	Aids blood clotting over wounds	Most vegetables
MINERALS		
Sodium*	Helps maintain body's water balance and enables nerves and muscles to function properly	Salt added to foods during preparation at home or in factories
Potassium	Works with sodium to maintain water balance and enables nerves and muscles to function	Most fruits and vegetables
Calcium	Helps form bones and teeth. Enables muscles to contract. Blood calcium promotes efficient clotting over wounds	All milks, hard cheeses, white bread and flour, spinach, chick peas, other vegetables, figs, sardines
Iron	Helps form healthy red blood cells. Enables the body to use food energy	Liver, kidney, lean beef, chocolate, all breads
Fluorine	Strengthens teeth against decay	Drinking water, tea, sardines. Also present in fluoride toothpastes

Many other minerals are needed in tiny amounts. As long as the diet contains many different foods and provides enough energy (measured in calories or kilojoules) and enough fibre, protein and vitamins, it will also provide enough of all the trace minerals.

WHERE IS THE ENERGY IN FOOD?

Energy is not a nutrient. It cannot exist on its own but is an integral part of proteins, fats, starches, sugars and alcohol (which is not an essential nutrient but is high in calories).

Energy is measured in Calories or kilojoules. If you see 'kcals' on a label it's the same as 'Calories'.

The energy value of nutrients is not the same:

1g fat supplies 9 Calories (37 kJ or kilojoules)
1g alcohol has 7 Calories (29 kJ)
1g protein has 4 Calories (17 kJ)
1g starch has 3.75 Calories (16 kJ)
1g any sugar has 3.75 Calories (16 kJ)

Clearly, it is likely that a food which has a lot of fat will be high in calories.

The table shows that many nutrients are found in lots of different foods. It also shows that most foods contain a whole range of nutrients. So it is meaningless to talk of meat as just a protein food or of bread only as a starchy food. Meat contains several B group vitamins and iron as well as protein. Bread contains protein, fibre and B group vitamins as well as starch.

> **EATING AS MANY DIFFERENT FOODS AS POSSIBLE IS AN EFFECTIVE AND EASY WAY OF MAKING SURE WE EAT ALL THE NUTRIENTS FOR HEALTH.**
> **EATING ENOUGH TO BE THE RIGHT WEIGHT MEANS WE'LL GET ENOUGH OF ALL THESE NUTRIENTS**

This is a very good general rule. It needs to be modified a bit, but we'll deal with that later, when we talk about fat, salt and fibre. Fortunately, there is no need to sit down with a calculator and tot up the amount of every nutrient we eat each day! With the vast majority of nutrients, any we eat in excess of what we need is either excreted or simply not absorbed. The exceptions are proteins, fats, starches, sugars and alcohol. Eating too much of any of these usually results in obesity because they are converted to body fat and stored.

Huge doses of vitamin A and vitamin D can be poisonous, but usually it's impossible to overdose just by eating food. However, a man who was addicted to carrot juice was in the habit of drinking eight pints a day. He turned yellow and died of vitamin A poisoning! And it's certainly unwise to overdo vitamin tablets.

WHY ALL THE FUSS ABOUT THE WAY WE EAT?

Let's get one thing straight. *Eating is good for you.* If you don't eat you die.

The vitamin deficiency diseases, such as scurvy (lack of vitamin C) and rickets (lack of vitamin D) which used to be quite common in Britain, are now a rarity. An underfed child is so unusual we usually hear about it in national newspapers. More and more people are living to be eighty and older. So what's all the fuss about? Why do we see headlines such as 'Fat is a killer', 'Digging our graves with our teeth', 'Health warning — the food you eat can kill'?

Since the 1970s, professional, media and public interest in the relationship between food and health has increased enormously. And, according to most newspapers, radio and television programmes, all the news is bad. So just how good are our diets? The truth is that some people, probably quite a high proportion of the total population, could benefit if they made some adjustments to their diets.

WHAT ARE THE MAJOR HEALTH PROBLEMS IN BRITAIN?

There are five conditions which concern the medical profession because they mean people are ill or dying prematurely. These are:

★ **Obesity**
★ **Heart disease**
★ **High blood pressure**
★ **Tooth decay**
★ **Cancers**

A brief glance at some facts will show why doctors are concerned.

★ *Half of all middle-aged men and over one-third of women in the same age group are too fat. Being too fat increases the risk of*
    — having high blood pressure
    — having a heart attack
    — getting diabetes in middle-age
Quite apart from the health problems which may be faced by overweight people, fatness is simply not fashionable any more.

★ *Britain has just about the highest rate of heart disease in the world. In 1980 about 140,000 people (mainly men) died of heart disease in this country. One-third of those deaths occurred prematurely, ie before retiring age.*

★ *People who have high blood pressure (hypertension) are more likely than others to have a heart attack or stroke. No one knows how many adults have high blood pressure. Estimates vary from 15% to 40%.*

★ *Nearly 30% of adults have no natural teeth left. Nearly half of all five year olds have some decayed or filled teeth. This is a dramatic improvement since 1973 when almost three-quarters of five year olds had some decay. But there's still room for further improvement.*

★ *There are many different cancers but, as a group, they account for over one-fifth of all deaths.*

★ *Up to half of all elderly people regularly take laxative drugs. These can be habit-forming and may lead to poor absorption of some nutrients.*

WHAT PART CAN DIET PLAY IN MAKING PEOPLE HEALTHIER?

This, of course, is the question that has been taxing researchers and the medical profession for years. And it does seem that the right diet may provide part of the answer.

★ *There is no doubt that eating properly can prevent and cure obesity.*

★ *The correct diet is one factor which can probably reduce heart disease.*

★ *Diet may play some role in causing and curing high blood pressure.*

★ *Our choice of food and the way we eat it are two of the three important factors determining the health of our teeth. The third, of course, is regular and thorough cleaning.*

★ *Eating properly may play a part in preventing a small number of cancers.*

★ *The right diet can prevent or cure almost all cases of simple constipation and virtually eliminate the need for laxative drugs.*

WHY DO SOME PEOPLE GET FAT?

There are some fortunate people who seem to be able to eat an enormous number of calories and not gain any weight. Somehow they get rid of the excess. Others manage to control calorie intake and take in just enough to cater for their needs. But a large number of people tend to eat more than they need and to store the surplus as fat. Why there should be these three categories of people is a mystery. But we do know how people can slim and, with conscious effort, not get fat in the first place.

THE FACTS ABOUT SLIMMING

If you eat fewer calories than you use, you are bound to lose weight. To slim you have to eat less or use more calories or both. Almost every overweight woman will lose weight steadily at an average of 2lb/1kg a week by eating 1200 to 1400 Calories a day. For the majority of men and teenagers the figure is 1400 to 1600 Calories a day.

It is very difficult to lose weight by eating the same and taking more exercise. But being more active *and* cutting calorie intake is ideal. Exercise tones muscles and improves body shape.

No food is inherently fattening or slimming. What matters is the total number of calories eaten day after day. There is no magic food or pill that will melt body fat.

A healthy slimming diet contains many different foods. The best way to cut calories, improve general health and feel satisfied after eating is to cut down on the very high fat foods, many of which are also high in sugar and low in water and therefore contain a lot of calories for their weight.

The truth is that no one needs to look at height and weight charts to see whether they are too fat. A mirror and a good pinch of honesty are quite enough. However, for those who want confirmation, find your height on the chart opposite and see whether you need to lose a few pounds — or more. The chart may be used by both men and women.

> **ALL MEDICAL AUTHORITIES AGREE THAT IT IS UNHEALTHY TO BE TOO FAT. BEING JUST A BIT TOO FAT IS BAD, ESPECIALLY FOR YOUNG PEOPLE**

Help yourself to slim healthily and effectively.

★ *Try to keep to three meals a day and very little between.*
★ *Eat slowly.*
★ *Drink plenty of water and low-calorie drinks.*
★ *Change to skimmed or low-fat milk.*
★ *Use a sugar substitute in drinks and for some cooked dishes.*
★ *Cut all visible fat from meat.*
★ *Count calories carefully. At the start of your slimming programme it may help to weigh food so you know you are keeping to your prescribed calorie intake.*
★ *Spread butter/margarine very thinly.*
★ *Eat plenty of vegetables.*
★ *Have fruit for pudding.*
★ *Be determined and patient!*
★ *Decide to enjoy slimming and don't feel deprived.*

WHAT CAUSES HEART DISEASE?

The simple, honest answer is that no one knows. From all that has been written in newspapers and magazines you might think that the causes and prevention of heart disease are clear. They are not. However, a great many eminent doctors and researchers believe there is enough good evidence to justify a change of diet.

Hundreds of experiments and trials have been undertaken in many countries including the USA and UK, Finland and Norway. In some, researchers have observed the number of people who have a heart attack and noted many aspects of their lifestyle including smoking habits, fat consumption, blood cholesterol level, body weight, exercise pattern, blood pressure and family history.

The results of all the studies show:

★ *Heart disease tends to run in families. There is no doubt that genetically some people are more likely than others to have a heart attack.*

★ *Fat people are more likely than slim people to get heart disease.*

★ *Communities in which blood cholesterol levels are high have higher rates of heart disease than communities with low cholesterol levels.*

★ *In groups with a high fat intake there will be more heart attacks than in groups which eat less fat, especially less saturated fat.*

★ *Communities where many people have high blood pressure have higher rates of heart disease.*

★ *More smokers than non-smokers have heart attacks.*

★ *There are fewer heart attacks among people who are physically active than among those who lead a sedentary life.*

All this may sound pretty convincing. But it doesn't *prove* that obesity or high blood cholesterol or a high fat intake or high blood pressure or inactivity actually cause heart disease. Neither does it *prove* that correcting any or all of these disorders will protect every individual from heart disease. Nevertheless, almost every expert committee in the world which has studied heart disease has said the results of all trials suggest that the chances of having a heart attack will be reduced if people eat less fat, stay or get slim, prevent or correct high blood pressure, take enough exercise and don't smoke.

Even the few doctors who are not convinced about the relation between fat and heart disease admit that being overweight is bad for health and that eating less fat is a good way to lose weight.

In the UK, an eminent committee of doctors and researchers produced a report* which recommended that no one should eat more than 35% of their energy as fat. On average, in 1983, fat contributed over 40% of all our calories. The reduction, they said, should come mainly by eating less saturated fat.

WAYS TO EAT LESS SATURATED FAT

★ *Change from whole to skimmed or low-fat milk. (This does not apply to under fives.)*

★ *Spread butter or margarine very thinly but eat some polyunsaturated margarine.*

★ *Cut all visible fat from meat and discard chicken skin.*

★ *Grill food without fat instead of frying it.*

★ *Eat less prepared meat and pastry products, but eat more white and oily fish. (It's a good idea to eat some oily fish because varieties such as herring, kippers and mackerel contain polyunsaturated fats which not only tend to lower blood cholesterol but also help to prevent blood forming clots in the heart's arteries. In other words, oily fish could actually help to prevent heart disease.)*

*The Committee on Medical Aspects of Food Policy 1984 report — 'Diet and Cardiovascular Disease'.

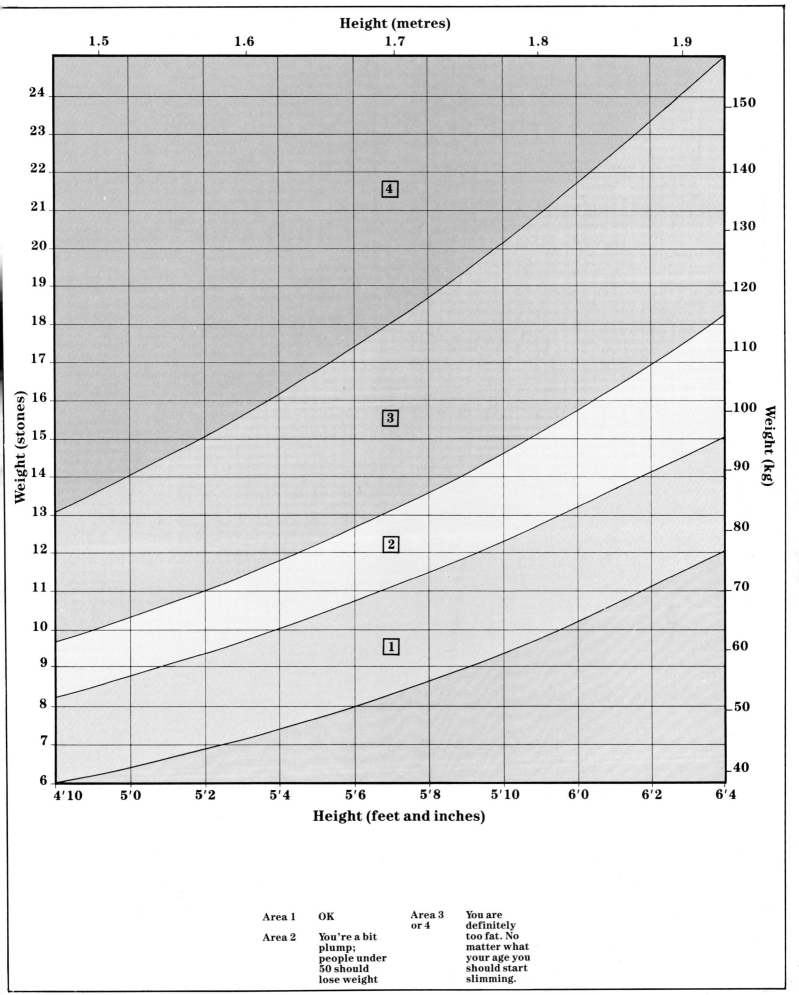

Area 1   OK

Area 2   You're a bit plump; people under 50 should lose weight

Area 3 or 4   You are definitely too fat. No matter what your age you should start slimming.

DOES SALT CAUSE HIGH BLOOD PRESSURE?

Everyone needs to eat some salt — it plays an essential part in maintaining the body's water balance. It also enables nerve impulses to trigger muscle contraction.

The amount we actually need is only about 0.5g a day, or less. Many people eat twenty times that much. Does it matter?

Most people have very efficient kidneys which excrete excess salt. But some people seem to be sensitive to salt. For them, a high intake may contribute to or worsen high blood pressure. Conversely, reducing salt intake helps some people to reduce hypertension. A great deal remains to be discovered about the role of diet in high blood pressure, but recent work suggests that potassium may be a kind of antidote to sodium. Eating *more* potassium in fruits and vegetables may be beneficial.

What is certain is that high salt intakes are dangerous to very young children. And it could be that, even though children don't get high blood pressure, mothers may be laying the foundations for problems later in life by giving babies and children diets which contain too much salt.

> **OUR PRESENT VERY HIGH LEVELS OF SALT INTAKE DON'T DO ANY GOOD. EATING LESS MAY BE BENEFICIAL AND WON'T DO ANY HARM**

If we tried to eat only the amount of salt we *need,* food would be very unpalatable. So it is suggested that we just try to cut salt intake a bit. As a guide, about 6g a day has been suggested. For some people that's a big decrease, but it is achievable if the reduction is made gradually. You'll be surprised how easily you can get used to less salty food and enjoy it.

WAYS TO EAT LESS SALT

- ★ *Get out of the habit of sprinkling salt on food.*
- ★ *Use less salt in cooking — add flavour with herbs and spices.*
- ★ *Eat more fresh foods.*
- ★ *Cut down the very salty foods (some examples are given in the table below).*

SOME SALTY FOODS

	Amount of food	Salt (g)
Canned/packet soup	½ pt/300ml	3.5
Table salt	½ teaspoon	2.5
Baked beans	5oz/150g can	1.8
Kippers	1 small fillet	1.3
Sausage	1 large	1.0
2oz beefburger	1	0.9
Breakfast cereals with salt	1oz/25g	0.7
Meat extract	1 level teaspoon	0.6
Corned beef	2 thin slices	0.6
Bacon	1 streaky rasher	0.5
Bread	1 medium slice	0.5
Cheddar-type cheese	1oz/25g	0.4

This table shows clearly that many factory-prepared foods are very salty.

WHAT CAUSES TOOTH DECAY?

Although dentists are still very much in business, the state of children's teeth has been improving steadily since the 1970s. The main reason is the use of fluoride toothpastes and adequate fluoride levels in drinking water. It's interesting that the improvement has occurred at the same time that chocolate consumption has actually increased!

In fact, there are some surprising facts about tooth decay.

- ★ *A clean tooth, free from bacteria, cannot decay no matter what type of food is eaten.*

★ *Any carbohydrate-containing food is capable of causing decay. That includes bread, pasta, potatoes, apples, dates, raisins and sugary drinks as well as sweets and chocolates.*

★ *The number of times a day carbohydrate-containing foods are eaten is far more important than the total amount of sugar or starch eaten. Constant nibbling of carbohydrate-containing foods leads to more decay than eating the same food in one or two concentrated sessions. (But remember that the amount of sugar and starch does affect calorie intake!)*

★ *Cheddar-type cheese and nuts at the end of a meal help to reduce decay if you can't clean your teeth. Apples actually increase decay rather than clean teeth.*

The lessons are obvious. Children should get in the habit of brushing their teeth very *thoroughly* with a fluoride toothpaste at least once a day — one good clean is better than three half-hearted efforts.

Parents should dissuade children from nibbling carbohydrate-containing foods, and babies certainly should not be given syrup-filled comforters.

CAN DIET HELP PREVENT CANCER?

There are many different types of cancer. Most are caused by environmental factors and smoking but food may be involved in a small number.

At the moment it seems that fewer people might get bowel cancer if they ate less fat and more fibre. Dietary fibre makes food move through the digestive system quickly so that any cancer-producing compounds are eliminated rapidly.

The precise role of diet in cancers will become clearer as more research is done. In the meantime, a host of other benefits has been proposed for fibre.

IS DIETARY FIBRE ALL IT'S CRACKED UP TO BE?

So many benefits have been ascribed to fibre that one could believe it is the simple answer to all our health problems. It has been claimed that an adequate intake can cure constipation, help people lose weight, prevent gall stones, hiatus hernia and appendicitis, as well as help prevent heart disease and relieve the pain of diverticulitis (a disease of the colon).

Because fibre is not absorbed into the body it undoubtedly prevents or cures almost all cases of simple constipation. This is not as trivial as it sounds. Eating enough fibre could virtually eliminate the need for laxatives. The trouble with these drugs is that it is possible, especially for the elderly, to overdose, get diarrhoea and so lose valuable nutrients.

There is also good evidence that eating enough fibre can cure the pain of some large bowel disorders. The other proposed benefits *may* be proved to be real when more research has been conducted.

MANY PEOPLE WOULD BE HEALTHIER IF THEY ATE MORE DIETARY FIBRE

At present, the average fibre intake in Britain is about 20g a day. Many medical authorities believe this should be increased to *about* 30g a day for older children and adults.

WAYS TO INCREASE FIBRE

★ *Eat more fruits and vegetables, especially peas, beans and spinach.*

★ *Eat at least as much wholemeal bread as white.*

★ *Eat a high-fibre breakfast cereal.*

GETTING IT ALL TOGETHER

There's a lot of advice about eating properly to promote maximum health. And many food producers are eager to tell you the specific benefits of their products. The trouble is that most of the information is fragmented and can be very difficult to put together to construct a total healthy eating plan. It gets even more difficult when you have to think what the different members of the family like eating.

But it isn't really difficult. It becomes easier when you realise that everyone in the family can eat the same kind of food. The guidelines for healthy eating are just as important for children as for adults. The whole thing can be boiled down to a few points.

★ *Don't be daunted by the prospect of eating differently. Make changes slowly and experiment to find the diet you enjoy.*

★ *Eat as many different foods as possible to get all the nutrients you need. Don't worry about the exact amount of fat and fibre you eat. On pages 78, 79 and 80 we've given figures to help you see which recipes and which everyday foods are low in fat and which are good for fibre so you get the general idea.*

★ *Be the right weight. If you need to, slim by cutting calories — aim for a total calorie intake of about 1200 a day for a woman, 1500 for a man or child.*

★ *Eat less fat, especially saturated fat, but continue to eat some polyunsaturated margarine and oily fish.*

★ *Eat more fibre by taking larger portions of fruits and vegetables and more wholemeal bread and other cereals.*

★ *Eat only small amounts of chocolate, sweets and savoury snacks. And don't nibble them throughout the day.*

★ *Cut down on salt and salty foods but don't make food so low in salt that it's unappetising.*

And remember that proper eating can do only so much. To be as healthy as possible, you should also take regular exercise at least three times a week and stop smoking.

Finally, do realise that no food is inherently healthy or unhealthy. What matters is the mixture of foods that is eaten. No food need be eliminated, but you may need to eat less of the fatty or high calorie foods and more of the high fibre foods.

We hope you'll use the information and recipes in this book to make interesting and healthy meals that everyone in your family will want to eat.

HOW MUCH FAT, FIBRE AND ENERGY?

There's no need to worry much about your intake of protein, vitamins and minerals. As long as many different foods are eaten, enough of these nutrients will be obtained. However, fat, fibre and, for some people, energy need attention. The amounts you should be aiming to eat are shown below, and on pages 78, 79 and 80 the listings of all the recipes in this book, as well as everyday foods, indicate the fat, fibre and calorie content of each.

FAT

Most authorities suggest that no more than 35% of all the calories people eat should come from fat. The recommended intake for different groups of people is shown below.

	Fat g/day
Children 5-7	60-70
8-9	70-80
10-12	80-95
Teenage boys	100-115
Teenage girls	75-90
Men	100-115
Women	75-85

People who are very active can eat more fat.

FIBRE

No two people *need* the same amount of fibre, or any other nutrient for that matter. But *as a very rough guide* it's a good idea to aim at eating about 30g fibre a day, less for young children. Never eat so much you get diarrhoea.

ENERGY

People vary enormously in their energy (calorie) needs. The best guide is your weight and the amount of flabby flesh around your waist. For those who need to slim, sensible goals for most people to aim for are:

Women	1200-1400 Calories a day
Men and older children	1400-1600 Calories a day

ABOUT THE RECIPES

Eating the right combination of foods is important for health. Equally important is that you still enjoy food. But even if you're not very interested in nutrition (why not?!) you'll certainly enjoy the new tastes and combinations of flavours in these recipes.

Some of the ingredients used may be strange to you, but nearly all are available from supermarkets. If you're adventurous you may discover flavours you enjoy.

Many recipes include freshly-ground black pepper. If you don't have a pepper mill you could use ready-ground pepper instead, although the taste won't be as good.

The amount of salt needed in each recipe has been carefully measured. If you find you'd like more you are probably eating too much. The best solution is to get used to less over a period of months, using a little less each time you cook. Because salt levels are low, many recipes include garlic instead. If you absolutely hate it, simply leave it out.

The main hard cheese in these recipes is Parmesan. Because it has such a good strong flavour only small amounts are needed and fat content is kept down. Freshly-grated Parmesan usually has a better flavour than cheese bought ready grated.

Many recipes use corn or sunflower oil because they are high in polyunsaturates. You could try soya oil or safflower oil instead. But avoid oils labelled 'blended' or 'vegetable' — they are usually not high in polyunsaturates. A few recipes include olive oil. Although it is not high in polyunsaturates, it does have a very special taste which is necessary in a few delicately-flavoured recipes. Using it occasionally, in dressings for example, is fine.

Again, for taste reasons, a few recipes include butter rather than polyunsaturated margarine.

Honey and demerara sugar are sometimes used because they have a better flavour than white sugar, not because they are any better for you than white.

Finally, just bear in mind the following three points and you'll get good results as well as delicious flavours.

* *All spoon measures are level not heaped.*
* *Oven temperatures are for conventional ovens. If you have a convection/fan oven you'll need to use the lower temperatures indicated in the manufacturer's handbook.*
* *Use either **all imperial** or **all metric** measures, don't mix them.*

SOUPS

Soups may be hot or cold, light or filling.
These recipes range from light Carrot and Celery Soup to substantial Minestrone,
which is a meal in itself. Try Chilled Avocado Soup on a hot summer's day

Prawn and Leek Chowder

SERVES 4

4oz	leeks or spring onions, sliced and washed	125g
½oz	butter	15g
4oz	peeled prawns	125g
1oz	lean boiled ham, cut in strips	25g
2pt	chicken stock	1 litre
	ground black pepper	
1 tablespoon	lemon juice	1 x 15ml spoon
12oz can	sweetcorn, drained	340g can
1	egg	1
¼pt	skimmed or low-fat milk	150ml

1 Cook leeks or spring onions in butter until tender but not coloured — about 5 minutes.

2 Add prawns, ham, stock, pepper and lemon juice. Cover and cook for 15 minutes.

3 Stir in sweetcorn.

4 Beat egg with milk and add a little at a time to the hot soup. Cook, stirring, for a few minutes. Do not allow to boil. Serve immediately.

Carrot and Celery Soup

SERVES 4

This soup does not require a lot of preparation
and is an ideal way of using up vegetables that may be a little soft.
You may find that it will need thinning with skimmed or low-fat milk.

8oz	carrots, washed and roughly chopped	250g
8oz	celery, washed and sliced	250g
4oz	parsnip, peeled and roughly chopped	125g
2oz	onion, chopped	50g
1 clove	garlic, crushed	1 clove
2 teaspoons	tomato purée	1 x 10ml spoon
	ground black pepper	
1	bay leaf	1
2½ pt	vegetable stock	1.5 litres
2 tablespoons	soured cream	2 x 15ml spoons
2 tablespoons	chopped fresh parsley	2 x 15ml spoons

1 Put all ingredients, except soured cream and parsley, in a large saucepan, cover and simmer gently for 30-40 minutes or until vegetables are soft. Cool, remove bay leaf.

2 Blend in a liquidiser or processor, or rub through a sieve.

3 Return to saucepan and heat through. Remove from heat and stir in cream just before serving. Garnish with parsley.

Freezing note. Freeze at the end of Stage 2. To use, thaw then complete recipe as above.

Paprika and Onion Soup

SERVES 4

1½lb	large onions, sliced	750g
2 cloves	garlic, crushed	2 cloves
2 tablespoons	corn or sunflower oil	2 x 15ml spoons
10oz	potato, scrubbed and finely chopped	300g
2 tablespoons	water	2 x 15ml spoons
4 teaspoons	paprika	2 x 10ml spoons
good pinch	caraway seeds	good pinch
2½pt	stock	1.5 litres
2 tablespoons	red wine vinegar	2 x 15ml spoons
½ teaspoon	salt (if unsalted stock used)	1 x 2.5ml spoon
	ground black pepper	

1 Gently fry onions and garlic in oil in a large covered saucepan.

2 Add potato and water. Cover and cook vegetables for 5 minutes.

3 Add paprika and caraway seeds and cook for 1 minute, then add remaining ingredients.

4 Boil, cover and simmer for about 30 minutes until potato has broken up and thickened soup. Serve hot.

Spinach and Potato Soup

SERVES 4

1	onion, chopped	1
8oz	potato, scrubbed and diced	250g
½oz	butter or polyunsaturated margarine	15g
1 tablespoon	water	1 x 15ml spoon
1lb	fresh spinach, washed, stalks removed	500g
	or	
8oz	frozen leaf spinach, thawed and drained	250g
2pt	stock or water	1 litre
1 teaspoon	dried oregano	1 x 5ml spoon
1 teaspoon	salt (if unsalted stock or water used)	1 x 5ml spoon
	ground black pepper	
2 pinches	grated nutmeg	2 pinches
2 tablespoons	soured cream	2 x 15ml spoons

1 Put onion, potato, butter or margarine and water in a saucepan, cover and heat gently until softened — about 5 minutes. Do not let the steam out.

2 Chop spinach and add to pan with all remaining ingredients, except cream.

3 Bring to boil, then simmer for 20 minutes. Blend in a liquidiser or processor. Just before serving, remove from heat and stir in cream.

Freezing note. This soup may be frozen without the soured cream, but soup takes up a lot of freezer space.

Spinach and Potato Soup; Prawn and Leek Chowder; Paprika and Onion Soup

Minestrone

SERVES 4

1 rasher	back bacon, lean only, finely chopped	1 rasher
½oz	polyunsaturated margarine	15g
1 large	leek, chopped and washed	1 large
2	carrots, washed and chopped	2
1 medium	courgette, topped, tailed and chopped	1 medium
4oz	green beans, topped, tailed and chopped	125g
2 sticks	celery, washed and chopped	2 sticks
2¼pt	stock	1.25 litres
6	ripe tomatoes, chopped	6
½ teaspoon	dried thyme	1 x 2.5ml spoon
½ teaspoon	dried basil	1 x 2.5ml spoon
6oz	white kidney beans, cooked or canned	175g
2oz	small pasta shapes, preferably wholemeal	50g
1 teaspoon	salt (if unsalted stock used)	1 x 5ml spoon
	ground black pepper	
2 tablespoons	grated Parmesan cheese	2 x 15ml spoons

1 Lightly fry bacon in margarine in a large saucepan.

2 Add leek, carrots, courgette, green beans and celery plus 3 tablespoons (15ml spoons) of stock. Cover and cook gently for about 5 minutes.

3 Add remaining stock, tomatoes, herbs, kidney beans and pasta. Season.

4 Boil, cover and simmer for 30 minutes. Serve hot, sprinkled with Parmesan cheese.

Chilled Avocado Soup

SERVES 4

8oz	low-fat cottage cheese	250g
5oz	low-fat natural yogurt	150g
1 small	ripe avocado, stoned and peeled	1 small
¾-1pt	skimmed or low-fat milk	450-600ml
½	small cucumber, grated	½
	ground black pepper	
	mint leaves	

1 Sieve cottage cheese and put in a liquidiser or processor with yogurt and avocado flesh. Purée until smooth and creamy.

2 Gradually add sufficient milk to give desired consistency, blend well.

3 Transfer to a large soup tureen or 4 individual soup bowls. Stir in cucumber and pepper. Chill well before serving, garnish with mint leaves.

Red Bean Chilli Soup

SERVES 4

4oz	onion, sliced	125g
6oz	carrots, washed and sliced	175g
6oz	swede or turnip, peeled and sliced	175g
2 sticks	celery, washed and sliced	2 sticks
1 tablespoon	corn or sunflower oil	1 x 15ml spoon
2pt	chicken stock	1 litre
3oz	dried red kidney beans, soaked overnight, drained	75g
1 teaspoon	chilli powder	1 x 5ml spoon
¼ teaspoon	ground cumin	½ x 2.5ml spoon
	ground black pepper	
2oz	Parmesan cheese, grated	50g

1 Put onion, carrots, swede or turnip and celery in a large saucepan with oil. Cover and cook for 5 minutes.

2 Add stock, beans, chilli powder, cumin and pepper. Boil for 10 minutes, cover and simmer for 1 hour.

3 Serve in soup bowls sprinkled with Parmesan cheese.

Watercress and Orange Soup

SERVES 4		
1oz	butter	25g
4oz	onion, chopped	125g
1 clove	garlic, crushed	1 clove
2 large bunches	watercress, trimmed, washed and roughly chopped	2 large bunches
2pt	chicken stock	1 litre
	ground black pepper	
1	orange, rind and juice	1
5oz	low-fat natural yogurt	150g
	grated nutmeg	

1 Melt butter in a large saucepan, add onion and garlic, cover and cook gently for 5 minutes until softened but not coloured.

2 Reserve a few watercress leaves and add remainder to saucepan. Cook for 3 minutes. Add stock, pepper, orange rind and juice, reserving a little rind for garnish. Cover and simmer gently for 15-20 minutes until watercress is soft. Cool.

3 Blend soup in a liquidiser or processor, return to saucepan to heat through. Just before serving, remove from heat and stir in yogurt. Alternatively, yogurt may be added to each bowl when serving. Garnish with reserved watercress, reserved orange rind, and a little grated nutmeg.

Freezing note. Freeze when cool omitting yogurt, which should be added after reheating and just before serving.

Clockwise from top left: Minestrone; Watercress and Orange Soup; Chilled Avocado Soup

PATES AND DIPS

Keep dips healthily low-fat by serving them with strips of
crisp raw vegetables such as celery, cucumber, chicory, carrot and peppers

Rosy Prawn Dip

SERVES 4

Use as a dip with crisp vegetables or put in tomato shells and serve as a starter.

2 large	tomatoes, peeled and deseeded	2 large
2oz	onion	50g
6oz	peeled prawns	175g
8oz	low-fat cottage cheese, sieved	250g
1 tablespoon	tomato ketchup	1 x 15ml spoon
2-3 drops	Tabasco	2-3 drops
½ teaspoon	paprika	1 x 2.5ml spoon
	ground black pepper	
few sprigs	fresh parsley	few sprigs

1 Put tomato and onion in a liquidiser or processor and blend until smooth.

2 Roughly chop two-thirds of prawns. Stir together tomato mixture, chopped prawns and remaining ingredients except parsley.

3 Mix well and chill. Garnish with reserved prawns and parsley.

Smoked Fish Paté

SERVES 4

A paté which may be made
with any cooked smoked fish such as mackerel,
trout, kipper or salmon.

2 slices	wholemeal bread, crusts removed	2 slices
8oz	cooked smoked fish	250g
5oz	low-fat natural yogurt	150g
2	spring onions, chopped	2
1 clove	garlic, crushed	1 clove
2 tablespoons	single cream	2 x 15ml spoons
1	lemon, grated rind and juice	1
	ground black pepper	

1 Soak bread in a little water, then squeeze dry. Discard water.

2 Skin, bone and flake fish.

3 Blend all ingredients, by hand, or in a liquidiser or processor until smooth. Press in serving dish and chill.

Avocado Dip

SERVES 4

1 medium	avocado, stoned and peeled	1 medium
4oz	butter beans, cooked or canned	125g
1 clove	garlic, crushed	1 clove
1	spring onion, chopped	1
½	lemon, juice only	½
½ teaspoon	salt	1 x 2.5ml spoon
2-3 drops	Tabasco (optional)	2-3 drops
	ground black pepper	

1 Mash avocado and beans. Stir in remaining ingredients. Blend until smooth in a liquidiser or processor.

2 Press in serving dish and chill.

Baked Tuna Paté

SERVES 6

2oz	onion, finely chopped	50g
2oz	mushrooms, washed and finely chopped	50g
½oz	polyunsaturated margarine	15g
7oz can	tuna in brine, drained and flaked	200g can
1oz	fresh wholemeal breadcrumbs	25g
5oz	low-fat natural yogurt	150g
1 tablespoon	tomato purée	1 x 15ml spoon
	ground black pepper	
1	egg yolk	1
3 tablespoons	single cream	3 x 15ml spoons

1 Pre-heat oven to 350°F/180°C/Gas Mark 4.

2 Fry onion and two-thirds of mushrooms in margarine until soft but not coloured. Remove from heat.

3 Stir in remaining ingredients and mix well.

4 Spoon mixture into 6 individual ramekin dishes, stand on a baking sheet and cook for 20-25 minutes. Garnish with reserved mushroom slices.

Vegetable Lentil Dip

SERVES 4

4oz	split red lentils	125g
½pt	cold water	300ml
1oz	butter or polyunsaturated margarine	25g
1 clove	garlic, crushed	1 clove
2	spring onions, finely chopped	2
2oz	mushrooms, finely sliced	50g
2oz	celery, washed and finely sliced	50g
1 tablespoon	chopped fresh parsley	1 x 15ml spoon
1 tablespoon	Worcestershire sauce	1 x 15ml spoon
1 tablespoon	lemon juice	1 x 15ml spoon
¼ teaspoon	salt	½ x 2.5ml spoon
	ground black pepper	
	celery leaves	

1 Put lentils in a saucepan with water, cover and cook for 20-30 minutes until thickened and water absorbed.

2 Melt butter or margarine in a saucepan, add garlic, spring onions, mushrooms and celery, cover and cook gently for 5-8 minutes until softened. Cool.

3 Put lentils and vegetables with parsley, Worcestershire sauce, lemon juice, salt and pepper in a liquidiser or processor and blend until smooth. Serve garnished with celery leaves.

Clockwise from bottom left: Smoked Fish Paté; Rosy Prawn Dip; Avocado Dip; Vegetable Lentil Dip; Baked Tuna Paté

SALADS

These salads are substantial enough to be eaten as light meals. Served as smaller portions many are good accompaniments to meat or fish dishes

Sunny Salad

SERVES 4

A crisp side salad or quick light meal.

4oz	green beans, topped and tailed	125g
1/3	cucumber, chopped	1/3
1 small bulb	fennel, sliced	1 small bulb
6	tomatoes, quartered	6
1	spring onion, chopped	1
8	black olives, stoned	8
6 tablespoons	Provencal Dressing (see page 29)	6 x 15ml spoons
3oz	Feta or Edam cheese, diced	75g
	ground black pepper	

1 Cut beans in quarters, blanch, drain and cool.

2 Mix all ingredients together.

3 Chill well and serve in a salad bowl or on 4 individual plates.

Pasta and Salmon Salad

SERVES 4

A tasty salad which is almost a meal on its own.
Ring the changes by using whatever salad ingredients you have available.

6oz	pasta shapes, eg shells, bows or twists, preferably wholemeal	175g
7oz can	salmon, drained and flaked	200g can
3oz	Edam or reduced-fat hard cheese, diced	75g
2 sticks	celery, washed and sliced	2 sticks
1/2	red pepper, deseeded and diced	1/2
2oz	button mushrooms, chopped	50g
4	spring onions, sliced	4
Dressing		
2 tablespoons	reduced-calorie mayonnaise	2 x 15ml spoons
2 tablespoons	low-fat natural yogurt	2 x 15ml spoons
1 teaspoon	French mustard	1 x 5ml spoon
1 teaspoon	lemon juice	1 x 5ml spoon
	ground black pepper	

1 Cook pasta in boiling salted water until just tender, 12-15 minutes for white, longer for wholemeal. Drain and cool.

2 Combine with remaining salad ingredients in a large bowl.

3 Blend dressing ingredients, pour over salad and toss lightly together.

Sunny Salad

Turnip, Date and Apple Salad

SERVES 4

An unusual combination of flavours,
this salad goes very well with cold chicken or turkey.

8oz	turnip, peeled and grated	250g
2	crisp green dessert apples, cored and diced	2
1 small	carrot, washed and grated	1 small
12	dried dates, stoned and chopped	12
1 tablespoon	lemon juice	1 x 15ml spoon
1 teaspoon	caster sugar	1 x 5ml spoon

1 Combine all ingredients in a large salad bowl.

2 Toss lightly in Orange Yogurt Dressing (see page 29).

Bean, Rice and Mushroom Salad

SERVES 4

4oz	dried red kidney beans	125g
4oz	long grain rice, preferably brown	125g
6 tablespoons	Provencal Dressing (see page 29)	6 x 15ml spoons
4oz	sweetcorn, cooked or canned	125g
1	green pepper, deseeded and sliced	1
2	spring onions, chopped	2
4oz	button mushrooms, sliced	125g
1 small	orange, juice only	1 small
½ teaspoon	salt	1 x 2.5ml spoon
	ground black pepper	

1 Soak kidney beans overnight, drain and discard water.

2 Wash and cook beans and rice separately. Make sure beans boil for at least 10 minutes, then simmer until tender. Drain and mix beans and rice.

3 While still hot, toss in dressing, cool.

4 Mix with remaining ingredients and chill.

Turnip, Date and Apple Salad; Bean, Rice and Mushroom Salad

Swedish Chicken Salad

SERVES 4

3oz	pasta shells, preferably wholemeal	75g
8oz	cooked chicken, diced	250g
1 small	green pepper, deseeded and diced	1 small
2 sticks	celery, washed and sliced	2 sticks
2oz	button mushrooms, sliced	50g
2	spring onions, chopped	2
2 tablespoons	reduced-calorie mayonnaise	2 x 15ml spoons
5oz	low-fat natural yogurt	150g
2 tablespoons	wine vinegar	2 x 15ml spoons
½ teaspoon	salt	1 x 2.5ml spoon
	ground black pepper	
1oz	flaked almonds, toasted	25g

1 Cook pasta shells in lightly salted boiling water until just tender. Drain and cool.

2 Mix all ingredients together except almonds.

3 Pile in a bowl, cover and chill for about 2 hours.

4 Sprinkle with almonds and serve.

Chinese Leaf and Beansprout Salad

SERVES 4

A crisp summer salad to serve on a hot day.

6 large	Chinese leaves, washed and shredded	6 large
4oz	fresh beansprouts	125g
1	red pepper, deseeded, halved and thinly sliced	1
2oz	unsalted peanuts	50g
2oz	sultanas	50g

1 Toss all ingredients together in a large bowl.

2 Serve with any of the salad dressings suggested on page 29.

DRESSINGS

Provencal Dressing has only a fraction of the fat
of traditional mayonnaise or vinaigrette;
the other dressings have virtually none

Orange Yogurt Dressing

MAKES ABOUT ¼pt (150ml)

5oz	low-fat natural yogurt	150g
1	orange, grated rind and juice	1
1 tablespoon	chopped fresh chives	1 x 15ml spoon
small pinch	grated nutmeg	small pinch

Put all ingredients in a liquidiser or processor and blend well,
reserving a little grated orange rind for garnish.

Tomato and Yogurt Dressing

MAKES ABOUT ¼pt (150ml)

4 tablespoons	tomato juice	4 x 15ml spoons
2 tablespoons	low-fat natural yogurt	2 x 15ml spoons
1 clove	garlic, crushed	1 clove
1 tablespoon	chopped fresh parsley	1 x 15ml spoon
½ teaspoon	caster sugar	1 x 2.5ml spoon
	ground black pepper	

Put all ingredients in a liquidiser or processor and blend well.

Provencal Dressing

MAKES ABOUT ⅓pt (200ml)

¼pt	tomato juice	150ml
2 tablespoons	red wine vinegar	2 x 15ml spoons
2 tablespoons	olive oil	2 x 15ml spoons
1 teaspoon	garlic, crushed to a purée	1 x 5ml spoon
½ teaspoon	mixed herbs	1 x 2.5ml spoon
	ground black pepper	
1 teaspoon	French mustard	1 x 5ml spoon

Blend all ingredients together until smooth. Store in a screw-top
jar in refrigerator.

Creamy Dill Dressing

MAKES ABOUT ⅓pt (200ml)

5oz	low-fat natural yogurt	150g
4oz	low-fat or skimmed milk soft cheese	125g
1 clove	garlic, crushed	1 clove
1 teaspoon	grated onion	1 x 5ml spoon
½ teaspoon	dried dill weed	1 x 2.5ml spoon
2 teaspoons	white wine vinegar	1 x 10ml spoon
1 teaspoon	horseradish sauce	1 x 5ml spoon

Blend all ingredients together until smooth. Store in a screw-top
jar in refrigerator for up to 1 week.

Orange Yogurt Dressing

TOAST TOPPINGS

Everyone loves toasted open sandwiches and the variety of toppings is enormous.
Some are quick and easy enough for children
to make so they won't need to resort to bread and jam

Devilled Kidney Toasts

SERVES 2

The Worcestershire sauce and mustard
add a spicy flavour to these kidney toasts — a really quick teatime snack.

4	lambs' kidneys, skinned, cored and quartered	4
½oz	polyunsaturated margarine	15g
1 tablespoon	Worcestershire sauce	1 x 15ml spoon
1 tablespoon	tomato ketchup	1 x 15ml spoon
1 teaspoon	made English mustard	1 x 5ml spoon
2 slices	wholemeal bread, freshly toasted	2 slices
	or	
2	white baps, split and freshly toasted	2

1 Fry kidneys quickly in margarine until lightly browned.

2 Stir in Worcestershire sauce, ketchup and mustard and cook for a further 2-3 minutes over a low heat.

3 Serve on toasted bread or baps.

Chicken and Corn Grills

SERVES 2

4oz	cold cooked chicken, no skin	125g
3 tablespoons	sweetcorn, cooked or canned	3 x 15ml spoons
1 tablespoon	reduced-calorie mayonnaise	1 x 15ml spoon
pinch	curry powder	pinch
1 teaspoon	dry sherry (optional)	1 x 5ml spoon
pinch	salt	pinch
	ground black pepper	
2 thick slices	bread, freshly toasted	2 thick slices
2oz	Edam cheese, grated	50g

1 Dice chicken and mix with sweetcorn, mayonnaise, curry powder and sherry, if used. Season lightly.

2 Spread topping on toast and sprinkle with cheese.

3 Grill to melt and serve immediately.

Prawn and Mushroom Toasts

SERVES 2

4oz	button mushrooms, sliced	125g
2 tablespoons	water	2 x 15ml spoons
small knob	polyunsaturated margarine	small knob
4oz	peeled prawns	125g
1	spring onion, chopped	1
	ground black pepper	
½ teaspoon	lemon juice	1 x 2.5ml spoon
2 tablespoons	soured cream	2 x 15ml spoons
2 thick slices	wholemeal or rye bread, freshly toasted	2 thick slices
few sprigs	watercress	few sprigs

1 Put mushrooms, water and margarine in a small saucepan, cover and cook gently for 2-3 minutes. Uncover and continue to cook to evaporate liquid.

2 Add prawns, spring onion, pepper and lemon juice. Heat through.

3 Remove from heat and stir in cream.

4 Pile mixture on toast and serve immediately, garnished with watercress.

Two-Bean Rarebit

SERVES 4

Originating in America, this snack is easy to make and
delicious to eat. Children love it served for lunch or supper.

2 teaspoons	corn or sunflower oil	1 x 10ml spoon
1 medium	onion, finely chopped	1 medium
1 clove	garlic, crushed	1 clove
1 small	green pepper, deseeded and chopped (optional)	1 small
7oz can	red kidney beans, drained	200g can
7oz can	baked beans	200g can
1 tablespoon	tomato ketchup	1 x 15ml spoon
2 teaspoons	Worcestershire sauce	1 x 10ml spoon
½ teaspoon	chilli powder (optional)	1 x 2.5ml spoon
	ground black pepper	
3oz	reduced-fat hard cheese, grated	75g
4 slices	wholemeal bread, freshly toasted	4 slices

1 Heat oil in a saucepan, add onion, garlic and green pepper if using. Fry gently until onion is soft but not browned.

2 Add kidney beans, baked beans, ketchup, Worcestershire sauce, chilli powder if using, and pepper. Heat through, stirring.

3 Add cheese and stir until melted. Serve immediately on toast.

Fluffy Tuna Baps

SERVES 2

3½oz can	tuna in brine, drained	100g can
1 tablespoon	reduced-calorie mayonnaise	1 x 15ml spoon
1 tablespoon	low-fat natural yogurt	1 x 15ml spoon
1	spring onion, chopped	1
1	egg, separated	1
	ground black pepper	
2	long wholemeal baps	2
few leaves	lettuce	few leaves

1 Pre-heat oven to 400°F/200°C/Gas Mark 6.

2 Mash tuna with a fork, add mayonnaise, yogurt, spring onion and egg yolk. Season with pepper.

3 Whip egg white until stiff but not dry. Fold into tuna mixture.

4 Split baps and pile tuna on cut surfaces. Bake for 10 minutes. Serve immediately, garnished with lettuce.

Devilled Kidney Toasts; Fluffy Tuna Baps; Prawn and Mushroom Toasts

Pizza Muffins

SERVES 1

1	wholemeal muffin or bap	1
1	tomato	1
1½oz	Mozzarella or Edam cheese	40g
1 thin slice	salami, chopped	1 thin slice
1	spring onion, chopped	1
4	black olives, stoned and sliced	4
½ teaspoon	dried oregano	1 x 2.5ml spoon
	ground black pepper	

1 Split muffin or bap and lightly toast both sides.

2 Slice tomato in 6 and put on cut sides of muffin or bap. Grill to soften for about 2 minutes.

3 Chop cheese and mix with salami and spring onion. Put on top of tomato. Grill to melt cheese.

4 Garnish with olives, oregano and black pepper.

Hot Liver on Rye

SERVES 2

1 tablespoon	wholemeal flour	1 x 15ml spoon
¼ teaspoon	salt	½ x 2.5ml spoon
	ground black pepper	
4oz	lambs' or calves' liver	125g
½oz	polyunsaturated margarine	15g
1 small	onion, thinly sliced	1 small
good pinch	dried mixed herbs	good pinch
½ small	lemon or lime, juice only	½ small
2 thick slices	rye bread, freshly toasted	2 thick slices
2 teaspoons	chopped fresh parsley	1 x 10ml spoon

1 Mix flour, salt and pepper.

2 Cut liver in thin strips and toss in seasoned flour.

3 Melt margarine in a frying pan, add onion and fry gently for 3 minutes.

4 Add liver and cook, stirring, for about 3 minutes until just tender. Do not overcook. Sprinkle with herbs and lemon or lime juice.

5 Pile on toast and garnish with parsley.

Mushroom Meringues

SERVES 2

4oz	mushrooms, sliced	125g
1oz	polyunsaturated margarine	25g
1	egg, separated	1
1 tablespoon	skimmed or low-fat milk	1 x 15ml spoon
1 teaspoon	made English mustard	1 x 5ml spoon
	ground black pepper	
2 slices	wholemeal bread, freshly toasted	2 slices
1oz	Edam or reduced-fat Cheddar cheese	25g

1 Sauté mushrooms in margarine until soft.

2 Beat egg yolk with milk and add to mushrooms. Cook gently until thick. Season with mustard and pepper.

3 Spread on toast.

4 Whisk egg white until stiff, spoon over mushrooms and sprinkle with cheese. Grill until golden brown. Serve immediately.

Soufflé Spinach Mushrooms

SERVES 4

These mushrooms look impressive when served,
but they are not difficult to make.
Choose good firm mushrooms not broken round the edges.

4 large	flat mushrooms	4 large
½ teaspoon	dried oregano	1 x 2.5ml spoon
	ground black pepper	
Filling		
8oz	fresh spinach, washed, stalks removed	250g
	or	
4oz	frozen leaf spinach, thawed and drained	125g
½oz	butter or polyunsaturated margarine	15g
1 small	onion, chopped	1 small
1 clove	garlic, crushed	1 clove
½ teaspoon	salt	1 x 2.5ml spoon
	ground black pepper	
½ teaspoon	grated nutmeg	1 x 2.5ml spoon
2oz	Edam cheese, grated	50g
2	eggs, separated	2
4 slices	wholemeal bread, freshly toasted	4 slices

1 Pre-heat oven to 375°F/190°C/Gas Mark 5.

2 Remove and chop mushroom stalks. Put mushroom caps in a lightly oiled flat ovenproof dish, sprinkle with oregano and pepper, cover and bake for about 15 minutes. Drain and keep liquid.

3 If using fresh spinach, put in a large saucepan without water, cover and cook for 1 minute. Put fresh or frozen spinach in a liquidiser or processor.

4 In the same saucepan, melt butter or margarine, add onion, garlic, mushroom stalks and cook for 5 minutes. Transfer to liquidiser or processor, add salt, pepper, nutmeg and any mushroom cooking liquid. Blend until smooth.

5 Return to saucepan, cool slightly, stir in two-thirds of cheese and both egg yolks.

6 Whisk egg whites in a large bowl and fold into spinach mixture.

7 Spoon on top of mushrooms, bake for a further 15 minutes.

8 Sprinkle with remaining cheese and serve immediately on toast.

Mushroom Meringues; Pizza Muffins

BURGERS

There's more to burgers than beef.
For a change, try fish, pork, chick peas or good Old Fashioned Rissoles.
They all freeze well too

Beefy Bran Burgers

SERVES 4

1lb	lean minced beef	500g
1 medium	onion, finely chopped	1 medium
½	green pepper, deseeded and finely chopped	½
1½oz	Bran Flakes, crushed	40g
2 cloves	garlic, crushed	2 cloves
2 teaspoons	Worcestershire sauce	1 x 10ml spoon
1 teaspoon	paprika powder	1 x 5ml spoon
few drops	Tabasco sauce	few drops
	ground black pepper	
4	wholemeal baps	4
	crisp lettuce leaves	
	cucumber slices	
2	tomatoes, sliced	2

1 Put all ingredients, except baps, lettuce, cucumber and tomatoes, in a bowl and mix well.

2 Form into 4 burgers using a 3 inch (8cm) plain scone cutter. Chill.

3 Cook under a hot grill or on a barbecue for 5-8 minutes each side, or until cooked and browned. Serve in halved wholemeal baps with lettuce, cucumber and tomatoes.

Freezing note. Freeze at the end of Stage 2, layered with greaseproof paper. To use, thaw and grill.

Pork Burgers

SERVES 4

1lb	very lean pork, minced	500g
2oz	onion, finely chopped	50g
1 clove	garlic, crushed	1 clove
1oz	fresh wholemeal breadcrumbs	25g
1 tablespoon	grated orange rind	1 x 15ml spoon
½ teaspoon	dried sage	1 x 2.5ml spoon
1 teaspoon	dried thyme	1 x 5ml spoon
	ground black pepper	
1	egg, beaten	1
2	tomatoes, sliced	2
4	wholemeal baps, split	4

Beefy Bran Burgers

1 Mix together all ingredients, except tomatoes and baps, using only just enough egg to bind.

2 Shape 8 burgers using a 3 inch (8cm) plain scone cutter. Chill.

3 Cook under a hot grill for 8 minutes each side until cooked and golden. Top with tomato slices and serve each on half a bap.

Freezing note. Freeze at the end of Stage 2, layered with greaseproof paper. To use, thaw and cook as required.

Nut Rissoles

SERVES 4

Any nuts may be used for these tasty rissoles. Almonds contain most fibre.

6oz	unsalted mixed nuts (hazelnuts, almonds and cashews), toasted	175g
4oz	celery, washed and sliced	125g
2oz	onion, roughly chopped	50g
2oz	carrot, washed and grated	50g
1oz	Parmesan cheese, grated	25g
3oz	fresh wholemeal breadcrumbs	75g
1 tablespoon	chopped fresh parsley	1 x 15ml spoon
¼ teaspoon	ground nutmeg	½ x 2.5ml spoon
¼ teaspoon	ground coriander	½ x 2.5ml spoon
	ground black pepper	
1	egg white, beaten	1
3 tablespoons	low-fat natural yogurt	3 x 15ml spoons
Coating		
1oz	white or wholemeal flour	25g
1	egg, beaten	1
2oz	natural bran	50g
2 tablespoons	corn or sunflower oil	2 x 15ml spoons

1 Put nuts, celery, onion and carrot in a liquidiser or processor and chop finely but do not purée.

2 Transfer to a bowl and mix in cheese, breadcrumbs, parsley, nutmeg, coriander and pepper. Bind mixture with egg white and just enough yogurt. Do not make mixture soggy.

3 With floured hands shape 8 rissoles, coat in flour, egg and natural bran.

4 Shallow fry rissoles in oil for 4-5 minutes on each side.

Freezing note. Freeze at the end of Stage 3, layered with greaseproof paper. To use, thaw, then complete recipe as above.

Smoked Fish Burgers

SERVES 4

8oz	smoked cod or haddock, cooked, skinned and flaked	250g
2oz	mushrooms, finely chopped	50g
1 small	onion, grated	1 small
2 sticks	celery, washed and finely chopped	2 sticks
2oz	fresh wholemeal breadcrumbs	50g
2 teaspoons	grated lemon rind	1 x 10ml spoon
1 tablespoon	chopped parsley	1 x 15ml spoon
	ground black pepper	
1	egg, beaten	1
2	wholemeal baps, split	2
2	tomatoes, sliced	2
few leaves	lettuce, shredded	few leaves

1 Mix all ingredients together with the exception of baps, tomatoes and lettuce. Use just enough egg to bind.

2 With wet hands shape 8 patties.

3 Grill for about 5 minutes on each side until nicely browned. Serve each on half a bap and garnish with tomato slices and lettuce.

Old Fashioned Rissoles

MAKES 8

8oz	cooked chicken	250g
4oz	fresh wholemeal breadcrumbs	125g
2 tablespoons	finely chopped fresh parsley	2 x 15ml spoons
1 small	onion, chopped	1 small
1	lemon, grated rind and juice	1
½ teaspoon	salt	1 x 2.5ml spoon
1	egg, beaten	1
2 teaspoons	Worcestershire sauce	1 x 10ml spoon
Crumb coating		
1	egg, beaten	1
3oz	fresh wholemeal breadcrumbs	75g
	corn or sunflower oil	

1 Mince or shred chicken finely, mix with all other ingredients except those for coating.

2 With wet hands shape 8 rissoles.

3 Dip rissoles in egg then breadcrumbs, shake off excess.

4 Pour ½ inch (1.5cm) oil in a frying pan and heat. Oil is hot enough when a cube of bread browns in ½ minute.

5 Fry 2 or 3 rissoles at a time for just long enough to seal. Turn and seal other side. Remove from pan and drain.

6 Put on a baking sheet and finish cooking under grill or in a hot oven (425°F/220°C/Gas Mark 7) for about 15 minutes.

Freezing note. Cool, pack and freeze after Stage 5. To use, thaw and cook under grill or in oven.

Chick Pea and Rice Croquettes

MAKES 8

Chick peas are tasty and a good source of fibre.

14oz can	chick peas, drained and rinsed	400g can
6oz	cooked rice, preferably brown	175g
1 small	onion, chopped	1 small
1 clove	garlic, crushed	1 clove
½ teaspoon	dried thyme	1 x 2.5ml spoon
1½oz	Parmesan cheese, grated	40g
1	egg, beaten	1
2oz	flaked almonds	50g
2 tablespoons	corn or sunflower oil	2 x 15ml spoons

1 Mash chick peas with a fork, then mix with remaining ingredients except oil.

2 With wet hands shape 8 patties.

3 Heat oil in frying pan, fry croquettes for 10 minutes, turning occasionally.

Serving suggestion. Serve hot in halved pitta bread envelopes or cold with crisp green salad.

Veal and Sweet Pepper Burgers

MAKES 4

These burgers are simple and quick to make.
The red pepper gives them a nice crunch.

1lb	minced veal	500g
	or	
1lb	mixture of minced veal and pork	500g
2oz	lean ham, chopped	50g
3oz	fresh wholemeal breadcrumbs	75g
½ small	red pepper, deseeded and chopped	½ small
1 small	onion, chopped	1 small
2 tablespoons	chopped fresh parsley	2 x 15ml spoons
1 teaspoon	dried oregano	1 x 5ml spoon
½ teaspoon	salt	1 x 2.5ml spoon
	ground black pepper	
4	wholemeal baps	4
½ medium	onion, sliced	½ medium
2	tomatoes, sliced	2

1 Mix all ingredients except baps, onion slices and tomatoes.

2 With wet hands shape 4 burgers.

3 Grill for 5 minutes on each side.

4 Put each in a halved bap with onion rings and tomato slices.

Freezing note. Freeze after Stage 2. To use, thaw and grill.

Chick Pea and Rice Croquettes in pitta bread with salad garnish; Smoked Fish Burgers

BAKES

Healthy eating doesn't mean never
eating cakes and biscuits. Carrot, Banana and
Walnut Loaf keeps well

Apple Drop Scones

MAKES ABOUT 12

1	sweet dessert apple	1
4oz	wholemeal flour	125g
4oz	plain white flour	125g
½ teaspoon	bicarbonate of soda	1 x 2.5ml spoon
1 teaspoon	cream of tartar	1 x 5ml spoon
1	egg	1
½pt	skimmed or low-fat milk	300ml
1 tablespoon	honey	1 x 15ml spoon
½ teaspoon	ground cinnamon	1 x 2.5ml spoon
1 tablespoon	corn or sunflower oil	1 x 15ml spoon

1 Coarsely grate apple, including skin.

2 Put all ingredients except oil in a liquidiser or processor and blend until smooth. Pour in a jug.

3 Put oil in a cup and have ready an old pastry brush (one you don't mind getting burnt). Heat griddle or large heavy-based frying pan until very hot. Brush lightly but thoroughly with oil.

4 Pour spoon (15ml spoon) batter for pan.

5 Cook a time and flip over when batter looks set and holes appear. Cook for a few seconds. Keep warm.

6 Cook remaining batter, brushing pan with more oil between batches. Serve immediately.

Freezing note. Cool and wrap carefully. To use, thaw and reheat gently.

Cottage Cheese Medallions

MAKES 15-20

4oz	wholemeal flour	125g
2oz	plain white flour	50g
1 teaspoon	dry English mustard	1 x 5ml spoon
½ teaspoon	cayenne pepper	1 x 2.5ml spoon
	ground black pepper	
3oz	butter or polyunsaturated margarine	75g
8oz	low-fat cottage cheese	250g
1	egg yolk	1
3 tablespoons	chopped fresh chives	3 x 15ml spoons

1 Pre-heat oven to 400°F/200°C/Gas Mark 6.

2 Mix all dry ingredients in a bowl. Rub in margarine until mixture resembles fine breadcrumbs.

3 Mix half cottage cheese and egg yolk together, add to dry ingredients, cut through with a knife and knead mixture to form a smooth, soft dough. Leave to rest for 30 minutes.

4 Roll out pastry on a lightly floured surface and, using a 1½ inch (4cm) plain cutter, cut out 30-40 biscuits.

5 Put on a baking sheet and cook for 8-10 minutes until golden brown. Cool on a wire rack.

6 Add chives to remaining cottage cheese and use to sandwich biscuits together.

Freezing note. Freeze after Stage 4, interleaved with greaseproof paper. To use, thaw and bake as above.

Carrot, Banana and Walnut Loaf

MAKES ONE 2lb (1kg) LOAF

4oz	wholemeal flour	125g
4oz	plain white flour	125g
2 teaspoons	baking powder	1 x 10ml spoon
1 teaspoon	bicarbonate of soda	1 x 5ml spoon
1 teaspoon	cinnamon	1 x 5ml spoon
7oz	carrot, washed and grated	200g
4oz	walnuts, chopped	125g
4oz	soft brown sugar	125g
1 large	banana, well ripened	1 large
2	eggs, size 3	2
1	orange, grated rind and juice	1
4 tablespoons	corn or sunflower oil	4 x 15ml spoons
4 tablespoons	water	4 x 15ml spoons

1 Pre-heat oven to 400°F/200°C/Gas Mark 6. Lightly grease a 2lb (1kg) loaf tin and line base with greaseproof paper.

2 Mix flours, baking powder, bicarbonate, cinnamon, carrot, walnuts and sugar in a large bowl.

3 In a jug, mash banana and whisk with eggs, orange rind and juice, oil and water. Pour on dry ingredients.

4 Beat together for a good minute to form a soft batter. Pour in loaf tin.

5 Bake for 50-60 minutes until firm, or until a skewer comes out clean when stuck in centre.

6 Cool in tin, then turn out and allow to get cold before slicing.

Garibaldi Biscuits

MAKES APPROXIMATELY 20

6oz	plain white flour	175g
2oz	wholemeal flour	50g
4oz	polyunsaturated margarine	125g
2oz	soft brown sugar	50g
1	egg, separated	1
1 tablespoon	skimmed or low-fat milk	1 x 15ml spoon
5oz	currants	150g

1 Pre-heat oven to 350°F/180°C/Gas Mark 4.

2 Put flours in a bowl, add margarine and mix with a fork until incorporated.

3 Add sugar, then bind to a soft dough with egg yolk and milk. Chill for 30 minutes.

4 Put dough on a floured surface and roll out to a large rectangle about ⅛ inch (3mm) thick.

5 Spread currants evenly over one half of pastry, fold other half over, press down and seal edges, trim.

6 Roll pastry sandwich until currants begin to show through top. Brush with egg white and cut in squares.

7 Put on a non-stick baking sheet and cook for 15-20 minutes until golden brown. Cool.

Apple Drop Scones; Carrot, Banana and Walnut Loaf; Cottage Cheese Medallions

FISH

White fish is particularly low-fat so it's good for slimmers.
Although oily fish has more calories, its fat is valuable because it is relatively unsaturated

Trout with Lemon Sauce

SERVES 4

1½lb	fresh spinach, washed and stalks removed	700g
	or	
12oz	frozen leaf spinach, thawed and drained	350g
4 small	trout, gutted and cleaned	4 small
½	lemon	½
½pt	fish or vegetable stock	300ml
1 small	onion, chopped	1 small
1 sprig	fresh fennel	1 sprig
	or	
pinch	dried fennel	pinch
½ teaspoon	dried thyme	1 x 2.5ml spoon
2 tablespoons	chopped fresh parsley	2 x 15ml spoons
1	bay leaf	1
¼ teaspoon	salt (if unsalted stock used)	½ x 2.5ml spoon
	ground black pepper	
1 tablespoon	cornflour	1 x 15ml spoon
1 tablespoon	cold water	1 x 15ml spoon

1 Pre-heat oven to 350°F/180°C/Gas Mark 4.

2 If using fresh spinach, cook for 2 minutes, chop. Put spinach in ovenproof dish.

3 Remove fins and, if you like, heads from trout. Lay fish on spinach.

4 Grate rind from lemon, squeeze juice.

5 Mix lemon juice, stock, onion, fennel, thyme, parsley, bay leaf and seasoning.

6 Pour over fish, cover and bake for 40-45 minutes.

7 Strain juices in a small saucepan. Mix cornflour with cold water and stir into juices. Stirring, boil to thicken and serve separately. Garnish fish with grated lemon rind.

Serving suggestion. Small boiled potatoes and grilled tomatoes.

Stuffed Mackerel Parcels

SERVES 4

1 small	onion, finely chopped	1 small
4oz	mushrooms, finely chopped	125g
2oz	fresh wholemeal breadcrumbs	50g
1 tablespoon	chopped fresh parsley	1 x 15ml spoon
½ teaspoon	dried dill weed	1 x 2.5ml spoon
½ teaspoon	ground coriander	1 x 2.5ml spoon
	ground black pepper	
¼ teaspoon	salt	½ x 2.5ml spoon
4 small	whole mackerel, gutted and cleaned	4 small
2	limes	2
	fresh dill or fennel (optional)	

1 Pre-heat oven to 400°F/200°C/Gas Mark 6.

2 Combine all ingredients, except mackerel, limes and dill, in a bowl and mix well.

3 Make shallow cuts along one side of each fish and stuff cavity with prepared mixture.

4 Put each fish on a large piece of aluminium foil. Squeeze one lime and slice the other. Pour juice over fish. Fold over foil to make 4 parcels and put on baking sheet. Bake for 30-40 minutes.

5 Serve garnished with slices of lime and a few sprigs of dill or fennel if available.

Serving suggestion. Boiled potatoes and mangetout or peas.

Seafood Cheesecake

SERVES 8

Base		
2oz	polyunsaturated margarine	50g
6oz	water biscuits, finely crushed	175g
2 tablespoons	low-fat natural yogurt	2 x 15ml spoons
1 teaspoon	anchovy essence	1 x 5ml spoon
1	lemon, grated rind only	1
	ground black pepper	
Topping		
8oz	low-fat cottage cheese	250g
3oz	low-fat or skimmed milk soft cheese	75g
3 tablespoons	low-fat natural yogurt	3 x 15ml spoons
1 tablespoon	tomato purée	1 x 15ml spoon
1 tablespoon	anchovy essence	1 x 15ml spoon
2 tablespoons	lemon juice	2 x 15ml spoons
2oz	crab sticks, roughly chopped	50g
	or	
2oz can	dressed crab, drained and flaked	50g can
6oz	peeled prawns	175g
1 tablespoon	powdered gelatine	1 x 15ml spoon
3 tablespoons	very hot water	3 x 15ml spoons
	ground black pepper	
	parsley sprigs	
½	lemon, sliced	½

1 To make base, melt margarine in a small saucepan, stir in all base ingredients and press in bottom of 8 inch (20cm) loose-bottom cake tin. Chill in refrigerator.

2 To make topping, sieve cottage cheese in a mixing bowl. Beat in soft cheese, yogurt, tomato purée, anchovy essence and lemon juice.

3 Stir in crab meat. Chop 4oz (125g) prawns and add.

4 Sprinkle gelatine on water in a small basin, stir to dissolve and add to fish mixture. Season with pepper.

5 Pour in base, smooth top and refrigerate to set.

6 Carefully remove from tin and garnish with remaining prawns, parsley and lemon slices.

Freezing note. Freeze in cake tin after Stage 5. To use, thaw, remove from tin and garnish.

Serving suggestion. Crisp green salad and boiled potatoes.

Trout with Lemon Sauce

FISH

Smoked Haddock Roulade

SERVES 4

Roulade		
2oz	plain white flour	50g
½pt	skimmed or low-fat milk	300ml
1½oz	polyunsaturated margarine	40g
pinch	dry mustard	pinch
½ teaspoon	salt	1 x 2.5ml spoon
	ground black pepper	
1½oz	Parmesan cheese, grated	40g
4	eggs, separated	4
Filling		
12oz	smoked haddock fillet, cooked, skinned and flaked	350g
1	spring onion, chopped	1
2 tablespoons	chopped fresh parsley	2 x 15ml spoons
4 tablespoons	low-fat natural yogurt	4 x 15ml spoons
1 teaspoon	horseradish sauce	1 x 5ml spoon
1-2 tablespoons	skimmed or low-fat milk	1-2 x 15ml spoons
	whole spring onions	

1 Pre-heat oven to 350°F/180°C/Gas Mark 4.

2 To make roulade, put flour, milk, margarine, mustard, salt and pepper in a large saucepan. Heat and whisk until thick. Simmer for 2 minutes and cool slightly.

3 Stir in cheese and egg yolks.

4 Line a 12 x 8inch (30 x 20cm) Swiss roll tin with foil. Oil lightly.

5 In a large bowl, whisk egg whites until stiff but not dry and fold into roulade mixture. Quickly spread in tin and bake for about 25 minutes until firm.

6 Put a sheet of non-stick baking paper or oiled greaseproof paper on a cooling rack. Allow roulade to cool slightly in tin then turn out. Carefully peel off foil.

7 To make filling, mix all ingredients except whole spring onions in a saucepan and heat gently, adding milk only if necessary to obtain a spreading consistency. Spread on roulade and roll up. Serve hot or cold. Garnish with spring onions.

Serving suggestion. Stir-Fry Winter or Summer Medley (see page 64) and a vegetable purée (see page 62).

Prawn and Corn Pancakes

SERVES 4

Pancake batter		
2oz	plain white flour	50g
2oz	wholemeal flour	50g
¼pt	skimmed or low-fat milk	150ml
¼pt	water	150ml
1	egg	1
pinch	salt	pinch
1 tablespoon	corn or sunflower oil	1 x 15ml spoon
Filling		
2	spring onions, chopped	2
1 large stick	celery, washed and sliced	1 large stick
1 tablespoon	corn or sunflower oil	1 x 15ml spoon
4oz	shelled prawns	125g
6oz	sweetcorn, frozen or canned	175g
4oz	low-fat or skimmed milk soft cheese	125g
	ground black pepper	
Topping		
1½oz	reduced-fat Cheddar cheese	40g
4 tablespoons	fresh wholemeal breadcrumbs	4 x 15ml spoons
	mustard and cress	

1 Blend all batter ingredients except oil in a liquidiser or processor.

2 Lightly oil an 8 inch (20cm) non-stick frying pan. Use batter to make 8 pancakes. Brush pan with oil before cooking each pancake.

3 To make filling, cook spring onions and celery in oil for about 5 minutes.

4 Add prawns, sweetcorn and soft cheese. Heat and stir until melted. Season with pepper.

5 Divide filling between pancakes, roll or fold each 'envelope-style' and put, fold down, on a serving plate.

6 Mix cheese and breadcrumb topping, sprinkle over pancakes and grill to heat and brown. Garnish with mustard and cress.

Serving suggestion. Salad of shredded white cabbage, toasted peanuts, orange and Creamy Dill Dressing (see page 29).

Fish Balls in Tomato Sauce

SERVES 4

12oz	haddock fillet, skinned	350g
4oz	peeled prawns	125g
1 teaspoon	chilli sauce	1 x 5ml spoon
1 tablespoon	chopped fresh parsley	1 x 15ml spoon
2oz	fresh white breadcrumbs	50g
1	egg white	1

Sauce

2	leeks, thinly sliced and washed	2
½oz	butter or polyunsaturated margarine	15g
2 tablespoons	water	2 x 15ml spoons
14oz can	tomatoes	400g can
4 tablespoons	dry white wine or cider	4 x 15ml spoons
½pt	chicken stock	300ml
½ teaspoon	dried basil	1 x 2.5ml spoon
½ teaspoon	salt (if unsalted stock used)	1 x 2.5ml spoon
	ground black pepper	

1 Purée haddock and prawns in a liquidiser or processor, add chilli sauce, parsley, breadcrumbs and egg white. Chill.

2 Meanwhile, lightly cook leeks in butter or margarine and water in a large covered saucepan for about 5 minutes.

3 Add remaining sauce ingredients, mashing tomatoes a little as they cook. Simmer for 10 minutes.

4 With wet hands shape 8 small fish balls.

5 Drop fish balls into simmering sauce. Poach for about 5 minutes.

Freezing note. Freeze sauce and raw fish balls separately. To use, thaw both and cook as above.

Serving suggestion. Tagliatelle or hot crusty wholemeal bread.

Prawn and Corn Pancakes; Fish Balls in Tomato Sauce; Smoked Haddock Roulade

POULTRY

Chicken and turkey are low-fat provided the skin is removed. They are
also very versatile. These recipes range from everyday
Chicken Pasta with Lemon and Tarragon to a rather special Chicken Lemon Soufflé.
In all these recipes, chicken and turkey are interchangeable

Turkey Fillet with Grapes and Peanuts

SERVES 4

1lb	skinned and boned turkey breasts	500g
1 tablespoon	corn or sunflower oil	1 x 15ml spoon
6	spring onions, cut in 2 inch (5cm) lengths	6
2oz	unsalted peanuts, ground	50g
8oz	green grapes, halved and seeded	250g
1½ tablespoons	soy sauce	1½ x 15ml spoons
2 tablespoons	water	2 x 15ml spoons
2 tablespoons	dry sherry	2 x 15ml spoons
	ground black pepper	
1oz	unsalted peanuts, toasted	25g

1 Cut turkey in thin strips. Heat oil in a large frying pan, add
turkey and cook quickly until beginning to brown.

2 Add spring onions and cook for a further 2 minutes. Add all
remaining ingredients, except for 2oz (50g) grapes and toasted
peanuts. Stir, cover and simmer gently for 5 minutes.

3 Serve garnished with remaining grapes and toasted peanuts.

Serving suggestion. Rice, preferably brown, and green beans.

Turkey Tandoori

SERVES 4

1lb	turkey breast fillets, without skin	500g
½ teaspoon	salt	1 x 2.5ml spoon
½	lemon, juice only	½
1 teaspoon	turmeric	1 x 5ml spoon
1 teaspoon	mild chilli powder	1 x 5ml spoon
5oz	low-fat natural yogurt	150g
1 small	onion, minced	1 small
1 clove	garlic, crushed	1 clove
2 teaspoons	grated fresh ginger	1 x 10ml spoon
1 small	green chilli, chopped	1 small
1 teaspoon	garam masala*	1 x 5ml spoon

1 Cut turkey flesh 2 or 3 times on each side.

2 Mix salt, lemon juice, turmeric and chilli powder. Rub mixture
well into both sides of turkey.

3 Blend remaining ingredients together until smooth. Ideally,
this mixture should be rubbed through a sieve, but it is not
essential.

4 Smear this mix all over fillets, put in a dish, cover and chill
overnight.

5 Pre-heat oven to 475°F/250°C/Gas Mark 9.

6 Drain turkey but do not scrape off yogurt coating. Put fillets on
a baking dish and bake for about 20 minutes until tender.

Serving suggestion. Crisp green salad and Indian bread or pitta bread or rice.

*Garam masala may be made at home by mixing the following:

pinch	ground cardamom	pinch
½ teaspoon	ground cumin	1 x 2.5ml spoon
¼ teaspoon	cinnamon	½ x 2.5ml spoon
¼ teaspoon	grated nutmeg	½ x 2.5ml spoon
pinch	ground cloves	pinch

Chicken Pasta with Lemon and Tarragon

SERVES 4

8oz	dried pasta shapes, preferably wholemeal	250g
1lb	boneless skinned chicken	500g
1 tablespoon	corn or sunflower oil	1 x 15ml spoon
2 tablespoons	water	2 x 15ml spoons
1	onion, sliced	1
2	carrots, washed and cut in sticks	2
1 tablespoon	wholemeal flour	1 x 15ml spoon
¾ pint	chicken stock	450ml
2 teaspoons	chopped fresh tarragon or	1 x 10ml spoon
1 teaspoon	dried tarragon	1 x 5ml spoon
1	lemon, grated rind and juice	1
4oz	button mushrooms, halved	125g
½ teaspoon	salt (if unsalted stock used)	1 x 2.5ml spoon
	ground black pepper	
2 tablespoons	soured cream or low-fat natural yogurt	2 x 15ml spoons
few sprigs	fresh tarragon or parsley	few sprigs

1 Boil pasta shapes in lightly salted water according to pack
instructions until just tender. Drain well.

2 Cut chicken in bite-size pieces. Heat oil in a large sauté pan and
fry chicken until lightly browned. Remove.

3 Add water, onion and carrots to pan. Cover and cook gently for
about 5 minutes, until softened.

4 Stir in flour and stock. Mix until smooth and thickened then
return chicken.

5 Add tarragon, lemon rind and juice and button mushrooms.
Season and simmer for about 10 minutes. Remove from heat.
Stir in soured cream or yogurt.

6 Mix in pasta shapes and serve hot garnished with tarragon or
parsley.

Turkey Fillet with Grapes and Peanuts; Chicken Pasta with Lemon and Tarragon

Chicken and Spinach Terrine

SERVES 6

An adaptable dish which may be
served hot with vegetables or cold with a salad.

1lb	uncooked chicken meat, without skin, minced	500g
3oz	onion, minced	75g
1oz	fresh wholemeal breadcrumbs	25g
2	eggs, beaten	2
3 tablespoons	low-fat natural yogurt	3 x 15ml spoons
1 clove	garlic, crushed	1 clove
½ teaspoon	dried tarragon	1 x 2.5ml spoon
¼ teaspoon	salt	½ x 2.5ml spoon
	ground black pepper	
8oz	frozen leaf spinach, thawed and drained well	250g
	or	
1lb	fresh spinach, cooked, drained well and finely chopped	500g

1 Pre-heat oven to 350°F/180°C/Gas Mark 4.

2 Put all ingredients, except spinach, in a large bowl and mix well.

3 Put one-third of mixture in a lightly oiled 1lb (500g) loaf tin. Carefully spread half the spinach on top. Add further layers finishing with chicken mixture.

4 Cover tin with lightly oiled aluminium foil, and stand in a roasting tin filled with water. Cook for 1½-1¾ hours until set. Leave to cool for a few minutes, then carefully turn on to serving plate. Serve hot or cold.

Freezing note. Cool and wrap. To use, thaw and reheat as required.

Chicken and Broccoli Flan

SERVES 6

Wholemeal pastry is easier to handle if the dough is quite moist
and left to rest in a cool place for at least 30 minutes before using.

Pastry		
6oz	wholemeal flour	175g
3oz	polyunsaturated margarine	75g
3 tablespoons	cold water	3 x 15ml spoons
Filling		
6oz	broccoli spears, washed and trimmed	175g
½oz	butter	15g
4 large	spring onions, chopped	4 large
8oz	cooked chicken, skinned and roughly chopped	250g
2	eggs	2
¼pt	skimmed or low-fat milk	150ml
2oz	Parmesan cheese, grated	50g
	ground black pepper	
1 tablespoon	sesame seeds (optional)	1 x 15ml spoon

1 Pre-heat oven to 375°F/190°F/Gas Mark 5.

2 To make pastry, put flour in a bowl, add margarine and blend in using a fork. Add water and bind to a moist dough. Knead lightly until smooth, wrap and chill for 30 minutes.

3 To make filling, remove thick stalks from broccoli, slice and add to salad, see serving suggestion below. Blanch florets in boiling water for 5 minutes, drain and cool.

4 Melt butter in a small saucepan, add spring onions, cover and cook gently for 3 minutes.

5 Roll out pastry on a floured surface and use to line a 9 inch (22cm) flan ring or dish.

6 Put broccoli florets around edge of flan case. Fill centre with spring onions and top with chicken.

7 Whisk eggs, milk and cheese together. Season with pepper, pour in flan case.

8 Sprinkle sesame seeds, if using, over top and bake for 30-35 minutes until set and golden brown. Serve hot or cold.

Freezing note. Freeze after Stage 7. To use, thaw, and complete recipe as above.

Serving suggestion. Baked potatoes and salad made with thinly sliced broccoli stalks, diced cucumber, chicory and Orange Yogurt Dressing (see page 29).

Chicken Lemon Soufflé

SERVES 4

This soufflé must be eaten as soon as it comes out of the oven.

1oz	polyunsaturated margarine	25g
1oz	white or wholemeal flour	25g
8fl oz	skimmed or low-fat milk	225ml
4	eggs, separated	4
4oz	cooked chicken meat, skinned and minced	125g
1 teaspoon	grated lemon rind	1 x 5ml spoon
2 teaspoons	lemon juice	1 x 10ml spoon
¼ teaspoon	salt	½ x 2.5ml spoon
	ground black pepper	
4oz	frozen mixed vegetables, thawed	125g

1 Pre-heat oven to 350°F/180°C/Gas Mark 4.

2 Melt margarine in a saucepan, stir in flour and gradually add milk, stirring all the time over a low heat until sauce thickens. Cook for 2 minutes.

3 Remove from heat, cool slightly, beat in egg yolks, stir in chicken, lemon rind and juice, salt and pepper.

4 Beat egg whites until stiff but not dry, fold into chicken mixture very carefully.

5 Put vegetables in a 2pt (1 litre) ovenproof soufflé dish and pour in soufflé mixture. Cook for 40-45 minutes.

Chicken and Spinach Terrine; Chicken and Broccoli Flan

BEEF

Lean beef contains only 4% fat.
But it is important to trim away all visible fat.
In all these recipes, pork or lamb
may be used instead of beef; well-trimmed
pork chops instead of rump steak

Fruity Beef Casserole

SERVES 4

Apricots add a fruity flavour to this warming casserole.

2oz	onion, roughly chopped	50g
4oz	carrot, washed and sliced	125g
1 clove	garlic, crushed	1 clove
2 tablespoons	corn or sunflower oil	2 x 15ml spoons
1lb	lean braising steak, cubed	500g
1oz	white flour seasoned with ground black pepper	25g
¾pt	beef stock	450ml
6oz	courgettes, topped, tailed and sliced	175g
3	tomatoes, quartered	3
3oz	dried apricots	75g
1 teaspoon	Worcestershire sauce	1 x 5ml spoon
1 teaspoon	tomato purée	1 x 5ml spoon
1 teaspoon	ground coriander	1 x 5ml spoon
¼ teaspoon	salt	½ x 2.5ml spoon

1 Pre-heat oven to 350°F/180°C/Gas Mark 4.

2 Soften onion, carrot and garlic in half the oil for 4-5 minutes. Remove from pan.

3 Toss steak in seasoned flour, add remaining oil to pan and cook meat until browned and sealed.

4 Add onion mixture, stock and remaining ingredients. Transfer all to a casserole, cover and cook for 1½-1¾ hours until meat is tender.

Freezing note. Cool then freeze. To use, thaw and reheat slowly.

Serving suggestion. Jacket baked potatoes and leeks or broccoli.

Pot Roast Beef

SERVES 4

2lb	slow roast beef joint, eg top rump, silverside	1kg
2	leeks, sliced and washed	2
4 sticks	celery, washed and sliced	4 sticks
2 large	carrots, scrubbed and sliced	2 large
1 tablespoon	French mustard	1 x 15ml spoon
1	orange, grated rind and juice	1
2oz	walnuts, chopped	50g
½ teaspoon	salt (if unsalted stock used)	1 x 2.5ml spoon
	ground black pepper	
½pt	stock	300ml
2 tablespoons	dry sherry or cider	2 x 15ml spoons
1 tablespoon	cornflour	1 x 15ml spoon
1 tablespoon	cold water	1 x 15ml spoon

1 Pre-heat oven to 425°F/220°C/Gas Mark 7.

2 Open roast beef for 20 minutes and drain off fat.

3 Reduce oven temperature to 325°F/160°C/Gas Mark 3.

4 Put joint in a large deep casserole, surround with vegetables. Spread mustard over meat. Add orange rind and juice, walnuts, salt, pepper and stock.

5 Cover and cook for up to 2 hours until meat is tender.

6 Slice meat and arrange on serving plate. Top with vegetables.

7 Put sauce from casserole in a small pan, add sherry and boil for 1-2 minutes.

8 Mix cornflour and water, stir into sauce to thicken. Pour a little over meat and serve rest separately.

Serving suggestion. Jacket baked potatoes and baked tomatoes.

Steaks with Orange Stuffing

SERVES 4

8 tablespoons	fresh wholemeal breadcrumbs	8 x 15ml spoons
2 teaspoons	chopped fresh parsley	1 x 10ml spoon
1 teaspoon	dried basil	1 x 5ml spoon
2 large	oranges, grated rind and juice	2 large
2	dessert apples, unpeeled and grated	2
1	egg, beaten	1
	ground black pepper	
4 small	rump steaks, all fat removed	4 small
2 tablespoons	corn or sunflower oil	2 x 15ml spoons
½ teaspoon	salt	1 x 2.5ml spoon
	orange segments and parsley to garnish	

1 Mix breadcrumbs, parsley, basil, orange rind and apple. Bind with egg, season with pepper.

2 Using a sharp knife, cut each steak horizontally to within ½ inch (1.5cm) of opposite edge, open out.

3 Fill 'pockets' with half orange stuffing, brush steaks with oil, season with salt. Make small patties with remaining stuffing. Grill meat and patties for 5-8 minutes on each side.

4 Heat orange juice and pour over steaks to serve. Garnish.

Freezing note. Prepare stuffing and freeze. To use, thaw, fill steaks as described above and grill.

Serving suggestion. Jacket baked potatoes and green salad with peas.

Steaks with Orange Stuffing

Pasticcio

SERVES 6

8oz	macaroni, preferably wholemeal	250g
Meat sauce		
1lb	very lean minced beef	500g
1 tablespoon	corn or sunflower oil	1 x 15ml spoon
1	onion, chopped	1
1 clove	garlic, crushed	1 clove
4	tomatoes, chopped	4
½pt	stock or water	300ml
3 tablespoons	chopped fresh parsley	3 x 15ml spoons
	ground black pepper	
2	egg whites, lightly beaten	2
Egg sauce		
¾pt	skimmed or low-fat milk	450ml
1½oz	wholemeal flour	40g
½oz	polyunsaturated margarine	15g
¼ teaspoon	grated nutmeg	½ x 2.5ml spoon
2oz	Parmesan cheese, grated	50g
2	eggs, beaten	2
2 tablespoons	wholemeal breadcrumbs	2 x 15ml spoons
	parsley sprigs	

1 Pre-heat oven to 350°F/180°C/Gas Mark 4.

2 Cook macaroni in plenty of lightly salted boiling water. Drain.

3 To make sauce, brown beef in oil, add onion, garlic, tomatoes, stock or water, parsley and pepper. Cover and simmer for 30 minutes. Cool slightly then stir in egg whites and macaroni. Transfer to a large casserole or baking dish.

4 To make egg sauce, put milk, flour, margarine and nutmeg in a saucepan and bring to boil, stirring. Simmer for 1 minute, then remove from heat and add three-quarters of cheese. Cool slightly and add eggs. Pour on top of macaroni mixture.

5 Mix remaining cheese and breadcrumbs and sprinkle on sauce. Bake for about 1 hour. Garnish with parsley.

Chilli Beef and Bean Pot

SERVES 4

12oz	braising beef	350g
2 tablespoons	corn or sunflower oil	2 x 15ml spoons
1	onion, chopped	1
1	fresh green chilli, deseeded and chopped	1
2 cloves	garlic, crushed	2 cloves
2 tablespoons	water	2 x 15ml spoons
4oz	dried red kidney beans, soaked overnight	125g
14oz can	tomatoes	400g can
½pt	stock	300ml
2 tablespoons	tomato purée	2 x 15ml spoons
2	bay leaves	2
5	cloves	5
1 teaspoon	dried oregano	1 x 5ml spoon
1 tablespoon	mild chilli powder	1 x 15ml spoon
½ teaspoon	cinnamon	1 x 2.5ml spoon
½ teaspoon	salt (if unsalted stock used)	1 x 2.5ml spoon
	ground black pepper	
1 tablespoon	malt vinegar	1 x 15ml spoon
1 teaspoon	cayenne pepper (optional)	1 x 5ml spoon

1 Trim beef and cut in small cubes. Brown in oil and remove from saucepan.

2 Put onion, chilli, garlic and water in saucepan, cover and simmer for 5 minutes.

3 In another saucepan, boil beans in fresh water for 10 minutes. Drain.

4 Add meat and beans to onion mixture, stir in all remaining ingredients, adding cayenne pepper if you like a hotter flavour.

5 Bring to boil, cover and simmer for 2-2¼ hours stirring occasionally. When meat is cooked, remove bay leaves and cloves.

Serving suggestion. Rice or bread and chilled cucumber with low-fat natural yogurt.

Spice and Nut Meat Loaf

SERVES 6

1lb	very lean minced meat	500g
4oz	fresh wholemeal breadcrumbs	125g
1 large	onion, chopped	1 large
2 cloves	garlic, crushed	2 cloves
1 tablespoon	curry powder	1 x 15ml spoon
2 tablespoons	desiccated coconut	2 x 15ml spoons
1oz	flaked almonds, toasted	25g
1 tablespoon	mango chutney	1 x 15ml spoon
1	egg, beaten	1
½ teaspoon	salt	1 x 2.5ml spoon
	ground black pepper	
5oz	low-fat natural yogurt	150g

1 Pre-heat oven to 375°F/190°C/Gas Mark 5.

2 Line base of a 2lb (1kg) loaf tin with aluminium foil. Oil lightly.

3 Mix together all ingredients except yogurt and press in loaf tin.

4 Cover with more foil, sealing tightly, and bake for about 1 hour.

5 Pour off fat, allow to stand for 10 minutes and turn out.

6 Serve hot or cold in slices, topped with yogurt.

Freezing note. Freeze after Stage 5. To use, either thaw and slice cold or return to loaf tin, thaw and reheat gently.

Serving suggestion. Wholemeal spaghetti or pasta shells, peas or green salad.

Chilli Beef and Bean Pot; Pasticcio

PORK AND LAMB

Lean pork and lamb are not the high fat foods some people imagine.
Lean pork has only 7% fat, lean lamb 9%. But do trim all excess fat away.
Curried Lamb with Chick Peas is particularly
high in fibre. Both pork and lamb are suitable for all these recipes

Portuguese Style Chops

SERVES 4

1 small	aubergine, sliced	1 small
1 teaspoon	salt	1 x 5ml spoon
1oz	polyunsaturated margarine	25g
1 medium	onion, sliced	1 medium
1 clove	garlic, crushed	1 clove
3 large	tomatoes, peeled and sliced	3 large
7oz can	cannellini beans, drained	200g can
½ teaspoon	mixed dried herbs	1 x 2.5ml spoon
	ground black pepper	
4	pork or lamb chump chops, all fat removed	4
	watercress leaves	

1 Put aubergine slices on a plate and sprinkle with salt. Leave for 30 minutes, rinse in cold water and dry on kitchen paper.

2 Melt margarine in saucepan, add onion, garlic and aubergine, cover and cook slowly for 10 minutes until softened.

3 Add tomatoes, beans, herbs and pepper. Cover and cook for a further 5 minutes.

4 Grill chops for 5-8 minutes on each side. Put on a serving plate, cover with vegetables and sauce and garnish with watercress.

Freezing note. Freeze after Stage 3. To use, thaw and complete recipe as above.

Serving suggestion. Courgettes and mashed potato.

Pork, Parsnip and Coconut Casserole

SERVES 4

1lb	lean pork, diced	500g
2 tablespoons	wholemeal flour	2 x 15ml spoons
2 tablespoons	corn or sunflower oil	2 x 15ml spoons
2 tablespoons	water	2 x 15ml spoons
2 cloves	garlic, crushed	2 cloves
1lb	parsnips, peeled and cut in large dice	500g
4oz	whole green beans, topped, tailed and chopped	125g
2 teaspoons	ground cumin	1 x 10ml spoon
1oz	desiccated coconut, toasted	25g
¾pt	stock	450ml
½	lemon, juice only	½
½ teaspoon	salt (if unsalted stock used)	1 x 2.5ml spoon
	ground black pepper	
3 tablespoons	low-fat natural yogurt	3 x 15ml spoons

1 Toss pork in flour, then brown in oil. Remove from pan.

2 Add water, stir up sediment and add garlic and vegetables. Cover and cook gently for 5 minutes.

3 Uncover, return pork to pan, and add cumin. Fry for 1 minute then add coconut, stock, lemon juice and seasoning.

4 Cover and simmer for 20-25 minutes until just tender. Remove from heat and stir in yogurt just before serving.

Note. Half the parsnip may be replaced with 8oz (250g) cooked or canned butter beans.

Serving suggestion. Rice or boiled potatoes and green cabbage.

Pork Tenderloin stuffed with Prunes

SERVES 3

1 x 12oz	pork tenderloin	1 x 350g
6 large	ready-to-use prunes	6 large
6	blanched almonds	6
1oz	lean ham, cut in strips	25g
2 tablespoons	chopped fresh parsley	2 x 15ml spoons
½ teaspoon	dried sage	1 x 2.5ml spoon
	ground black pepper	
Sauce		
¼pt	dry cider	150ml
½pt	stock	300ml
2 teaspoons	cornflour	1 x 10ml spoon
1 tablespoon	cold water	1 x 15ml spoon
½ teaspoon	salt (if unsalted stock used)	1 x 2.5ml spoon
	ground black pepper	
2 tablespoons	single cream	2 x 15ml spoons

1 Pre-heat oven to 350°F/180°C/Gas Mark 4.

2 Slit pork lengthways, almost through. Open out and put between 2 sheets of wet greaseproof paper and beat thin with a rolling pin or mallet.

3 Soak prunes in very hot water for 10 minutes and remove stones then stuff each prune with an almond.

4 Spread ham, half parsley and half sage on pork, season with pepper. Arrange prunes along centre and roll up firmly. Tie with kitchen string.

5 Put on a sheet of lightly oiled foil and wrap securely.

6 Bake for about 30 minutes or until tender.

7 Unwrap meat and strain juices in a small saucepan for sauce. Boil, add cider, stock and remaining parsley and sage.

8 Mix cornflour with water, stir into sauce and heat until thick. Season, remove from heat and stir in cream.

9 When meat has stood for about 10 minutes, slice, arrange on serving plate and pour a little sauce over. Serve rest separately.

Serving suggestion. Brussels sprouts and sauté potatoes.

Curried Lamb with Chick Peas

SERVES 4

12oz	lean lamb, diced	350g
1 tablespoon	corn or sunflower oil	1 x 15ml spoon
2 teaspoons	curry powder	1 x 10ml spoon
2-3 tablespoons	water	2-3 x 15ml spoons
1 large	onion, sliced	1 large
1 clove	garlic, crushed	1 clove
½ inch cube	fresh ginger, grated	1.5cm cube
8oz	chick peas, cooked or canned	250g
4oz	dried apricots, halved if large	125g
½pt	stock	300ml
½ teaspoon	salt (if unsalted stock used)	1 x 2.5ml spoon
½	lemon, juice only	½
	ground black pepper	
3 tablespoons	low-fat natural yogurt	3 x 15ml spoons
1oz	desiccated coconut, toasted	25g

1 Brown lamb in oil. Add curry powder and fry for 1 minute. Remove.

2 Add water to pan, stir in onion, garlic and ginger. Cover and cook for a few minutes until softened.

3 Return lamb to pan and add chick peas, apricots, stock, salt, lemon juice and pepper.

4 Bring to boil, stirring, cover and simmer for 40 minutes until tender.

5 Serve topped with yogurt and coconut.

Freezing note. Freeze after Stage 4. To use, thaw and reheat and complete recipe as above.

Serving suggestion. Brown rice or wholemeal bread rolls and any green vegetable.

Clockwise from top left: Portuguese Style Chops; Pork, Parsnip and Coconut Casserole; Curried Lamb with Chick Peas

VEAL

Veal is a special-occasion meat with a delicate flavour. But escalopes
are very thin and a little goes a long way. If you prefer, use
minute steak in place of escalopes and stewing beef instead of pie veal

Veal Mediterranean Style

SERVES 4

1oz	butter or polyunsaturated margarine	25g
1 large	onion, sliced	1 large
2 cloves	garlic, crushed	2 cloves
1lb	stewing veal, cubed, all fat removed	500g
4oz	button mushrooms	125g
1 large	green pepper, deseeded and sliced	1 large
8oz	aubergines or courgettes, cut in chunky fingers	250g
14oz can	tomatoes	400g can
¾pt	chicken stock	450ml
1 tablespoon	tomato purée	1 x 15ml spoon
1 teaspoon	dried oregano	1 x 5ml spoon
1 teaspoon	dried thyme	1 x 5ml spoon
½ teaspoon	salt	1 x 2.5ml spoon
	ground black pepper	
6oz	pasta shells, preferably wholemeal	175g
1 teaspoon	chopped fresh basil	1 x 5ml spoon

1 Pre-heat oven to 350°/180°/Gas Mark 4.

2 Heat butter or margarine in a large flameproof casserole, add
onion and garlic, cover and cook for 2 minutes until soft.

3 Add veal, cook until lightly browned. Add remaining
ingredients except pasta and basil, cover and cook in oven for 45
minutes.

4 Stir in pasta shells, cover and cook for a further 20 minutes until
pasta is tender. Check seasoning and serve. Garnish with basil.

Freezing note. Cool and freeze after Stage 3. To use, thaw, add pasta and
complete recipe as above.

Serving suggestion. Mixed green salad or green beans.

Veal Stroganoff

SERVES 4

A special-occasion dish which makes a little veal go a long way.

8oz	veal escalopes	250g
2 tablespoons	olive oil	2 x 15ml spoons
1	onion, chopped	1
1 clove	garlic, crushed	1 clove
6oz	button mushrooms, sliced	175g
2 tablespoons	water	2 x 15ml spoons
1 tablespoon	cornflour	1 x 15ml spoon
½pt	stock	300ml
2 tablespoons	dry sherry	2 x 15ml spoons
1 tablespoon	tomato purée	1 x 15ml spoon
1 teaspoon	dried dill weed	1 x 5ml spoon
½ teaspoon	salt (if unsalted stock used)	1 x 2.5ml spoon
	ground black pepper	
3 tablespoons	low-fat natural yogurt	3 x 15ml spoons

1 Slice veal thinly in strips.

2 Brown in oil then remove from pan. Add onion and garlic and
stir-fry until soft.

3 Add mushrooms and water. Cover and cook gently for about 5
minutes.

4 Sprinkle cornflour over mushroom mixture and stir in stock,
sherry and tomato purée.

5 Return veal to pan, add dill weed and season. Boil for 1-2
minutes to cook veal, then remove from heat.

6 Stir in yogurt. Do not allow to boil or sauce will curdle. Serve
immediately.

Serving suggestion. Boiled rice mixed with peas and diced carrots.

Fennel and Orange Veal Escalopes

SERVES 4

Fennel and orange add a delicious tang to veal. Choose thin escalopes.
Alternatively veal chops may be used, but these will require longer cooking.

8 small	veal escalopes (3oz/75g each)	8 small
	or	
4 large	veal escalopes (5oz/150g each)	4 large
1 tablespoon	corn or sunflower oil	1 x 15ml spoon
1oz	butter	25g
1 medium bulb	Florence fennel, chopped	1 medium bulb
4	spring onions, chopped	4
1 tablespoon	white flour	1 x 15ml spoon
¼pt	chicken stock	150ml
¼pt	dry white wine	150ml
2	oranges	2
½ teaspoon	salt	1 x 2.5ml spoon
¼ teaspoon	dried tarragon	½ x 2.5ml spoon
	ground black pepper	
2 tablespoons	single cream	2 x 15ml spoons
8oz	rice, preferably brown	250g

1 Fry escalopes quickly on both sides in oil and butter. Remove
from pan.

2 Add fennel and spring onions to pan and fry until soft but not
coloured. Add flour, cook for 2 minutes, gradually add stock and
wine, stirring. Heat until thickened.

3 Grate rind and squeeze juice from oranges. Add to fennel
mixture together with salt, tarragon and pepper. Return
escalopes to pan, heat gently, adding cream just before serving.

4 Meanwhile, cook rice in lightly salted boiling water, drain.

5 Place escalopes and sauce on a flat dish, garnish with sprig of
fennel, if available, and serve with rice in separate dish.

Serving suggestion. Broccoli with toasted flaked almonds.

Veal Mediterranean Style; Fennel and Orange Veal Escalopes

OFFAL

Many people don't like the taste of
plain liver and kidney. But in these recipes
other ingredients combine to give
delicious flavours

Kidney Creole

SERVES 4

1lb	lambs' kidneys, skinned and cored	500g
3 tablespoons	wholemeal flour	3 x 15ml spoons
2 tablespoons	skimmed milk powder	2 x 15ml spoons
2 tablespoons	corn or sunflower oil	2 x 15ml spoons
2 tablespoons	water	2 x 15ml spoons
1	green pepper, deseeded and sliced	1
1	onion, sliced	1
1 stick	celery, washed and sliced	1 stick
1 clove	garlic, crushed	1 clove
14oz can	tomatoes, puréed	400g can
2 tablespoons	red wine vinegar	2 x 15ml spoons
½ teaspoon	dried basil	1 x 2.5ml spoon
1 teaspoon	dried thyme	1 x 5ml spoon
¼ teaspoon	ground cloves	½ x 2.5ml spoon
¼ teaspoon	ground allspice	½ x 2.5ml spoon
½ teaspoon	salt	1 x 2.5ml spoon
	ground black pepper	

1 Roughly chop kidneys.

2 Mix flour and milk powder and use to coat kidneys.

3 Sauté in oil until browned then remove from pan.

4 Add water to pan, stir up sediment and add green pepper, onion, celery and garlic. Cover and cook gently for about 5 minutes.

5 Add tomatoes, vinegar, herbs, spices and seasoning. Bring to boil.

6 Return kidneys, cover and simmer for about 15 minutes.

Serving suggestion. Boiled rice or pasta and whole green beans.

Liver, Pea and Corn Risotto

SERVES 4

12oz	chicken or turkey liver, chopped	350g
1 large	onion, chopped	1 large
1 clove	garlic, crushed	1 clove
2 rashers	back bacon, lean only, chopped	2 rashers
2 tablespoons	corn or sunflower oil	2 x 15ml spoons
8oz	white long grain rice	250g
1½pt	stock	900ml
3 tablespoons	dry cider (optional)	3 x 15ml spoons
½ teaspoon	dried marjoram	1 x 2.5ml spoon
2 tablespoons	Worcestershire sauce	2 x 15ml spoons
½ teaspoon	salt (if unsalted stock used)	1 x 2.5ml spoon
	ground black pepper	
6oz	frozen peas	175g
6oz	sweetcorn, frozen or canned	175g
4oz	button mushrooms, sliced	125g
3 tablespoons	low-fat natural yogurt	3 x 15ml spoons

1 Sauté liver, onion, garlic and bacon in oil for about 5 minutes, stirring occasionally.

2 Add rice and fry for a further 2 minutes, stirring. Pour in stock and cider, if using.

3 Add marjoram, Worcestershire sauce and seasoning. Cover and simmer for 15 minutes. Add peas, sweetcorn and mushrooms.

4 Add a little water if necessary to keep just moist, cover and simmer for 5 minutes. Remove from heat and stir in yogurt.

Freezing note. Freeze before adding yogurt. To use, reheat gently, remove from heat and stir in yogurt.

Serving suggestion. Waldorf salad made with chopped apple, celery, walnuts and Creamy Dill Dressing (see page 29).

Leek and Liver Sauté

SERVES 4

1 tablespoon	corn or sunflower oil	1 x 15ml spoon
1lb	lambs' liver, cut in thin strips	500g
1 large	leek, cleaned and sliced	1 large
1 small	red pepper, deseeded and cut in strips	1 small
1 clove	garlic, crushed	1 clove
¼pt	chicken stock	150ml
1 tablespoon	tomato purée	1 x 15ml spoon
½ teaspoon	dried sage	1 x 2.5ml spoon
	ground black pepper	
2 tablespoons	medium sherry	2 x 15ml spoons

1 Heat oil in a heavy-based frying or sauté pan. Fry liver quickly on all sides. Remove from pan.

2 Add leek, red pepper and garlic to pan and cook for about 4 minutes only — the vegetables should remain crisp.

3 Return liver to pan and add remaining ingredients. Heat through and boil for 2 minutes. Serve immediately.

Serving suggestion. Noodles or pasta shells and green salad with red kidney beans.

Kidney Creole; Liver, Pea and Corn Risotto

MAINLY VEGETARIAN

You don't have to be a devout vegetarian to enjoy meals
without meat or fish. The extensive use of pulse vegetables and nuts makes
many vegetarian meals high in fibre

Lentil Bolognese Sauce

SERVES 4

1	onion, chopped	1
1 clove	garlic, crushed	1 clove
2	carrots, scrubbed and chopped	2
1 stick	celery, washed and chopped	1 stick
1 tablespoon	corn or sunflower oil	1 x 15ml spoon
2 tablespoons	water	2 x 15ml spoons
6oz	red lentils	175g
14oz can	tomatoes	400g can
½pt	stock or water	300ml
2 teaspoons	Worcestershire sauce	1 x 10ml spoon
2 tablespoons	tomato purée	2 x 15ml spoons
½ teaspoon	dried thyme	1 x 2.5ml spoon
1	bay leaf	1
½ teaspoon	salt (if unsalted stock or water used)	1 x 2.5ml spoon
	ground black pepper	
1 teaspoon	chopped fresh herbs	1 x 15ml spoon

1 Put onion, garlic, carrots and celery in a saucepan with oil and
water. Cover and cook gently for 5 minutes until softened,
stirring once.

2 Add remaining ingredients except herbs, bring to boil, stirring.
Cover and simmer gently for about 25 minutes until lentils are
soft. Add more water during cooking if necessary.

3 Remove bay leaf and serve garnished with chopped herbs.

Serving suggestion. Pasta or rice and celery and fresh bean sprout stir-fry.

Egg Foo Yong Omelet

SERVES 2

1 tablespoon	corn or sunflower oil	1 x 15ml spoon
1 clove	garlic, crushed	1 clove
¼ teaspoon	grated fresh ginger	½ x 2.5ml spoon
2	spring onions, chopped	2
2oz	fresh beanshoots	50g
2oz	button mushrooms, sliced	50g
1 tablespoon	dry sherry (optional)	1 x 15ml spoon
1 tablespoon	soy sauce	1 x 15ml spoon
3	eggs, beaten	3
2 tablespoons	water	2 x 15ml spoons
	ground black pepper	

1 Heat oil in a medium-sized frying pan. Stir-fry garlic, ginger
and vegetables for 1-2 minutes until just softened. Add sherry,
if used, and soy sauce. Stir and remove from pan.

2 Reheat pan, add a little more oil. Beat eggs, water and pepper.

3 Pour in hot pan and cook omelet until only just set.

4 Put vegetables in centre, fold over and serve.

Serving suggestion. Hot wholemeal rolls and crisp green salad.

Spiced Vegetable Bake

SERVES 4

1oz	polyunsaturated margarine	25g
1 medium	onion, chopped	1 medium
1 large	carrot, washed and diced	1 large
1 large	courgette, topped, tailed and sliced	1 large
4oz	mushrooms, sliced	125g
1 tablespoon	white flour	1 x 15ml spoon
2 teaspoons	curry powder	1 x 10ml spoon
½ teaspoon	ground cumin	1 x 2.5ml spoon
½pt	vegetable stock	300ml
1 tablespoon	tomato purée	1 x 15ml spoon
	ground black pepper	
6oz	wholemeal breadcrumbs	175g
2oz	Parmesan cheese, grated	50g

1 Pre-heat oven to 400°F/200°C/Gas Mark 6.

2 Melt margarine in a saucepan, add onion and carrot, cover and
cook for 8-10 minutes until softened.

3 Add courgette and mushrooms and cook for a further
3 minutes.

4 Stir in flour, curry powder and cumin. Cook for 2 minutes then
gradually add stock, stirring until sauce has thickened. Add
tomato purée and pepper. Transfer to an ovenproof dish.

5 Mix breadcrumbs and cheese and spread over vegetables.

6 Bake for 35-40 minutes until bubbling and golden brown.

Spaghetti alla Carbonara

SERVES 2

If you want to avoid all meat simply leave out the bacon.

4oz	spaghetti, preferably wholemeal	125g
2 rashers	back bacon, lean only, finely chopped	2 rashers
½oz	polyunsaturated margarine	15g
2	eggs	2
2 tablespoons	skimmed or low-fat milk	2 x 15ml spoons
pinch	salt	pinch
	ground black pepper	
pinch	ground nutmeg	pinch
1oz	Parmesan cheese, grated	25g

1 Cook pasta in plenty of lightly salted boiling water according to
directions on pack. (Wholemeal will take longer than white.)
Cook until it is still 'al dente', that is not soggy. Drain and keep
warm in saucepan.

2 Meanwhile, lightly fry bacon in margarine. Add to spaghetti.

3 Beat eggs, milk, seasoning and nutmeg. Add to spaghetti. Stir,
without reheating, until eggs are just set.

4 Serve topped with Parmesan cheese.

Lentil Bolognese Sauce with spaghetti; Egg Foo Yong Omelet

MAINLY VEGETARIAN

Pasta Pesto

SERVES 2

1 medium	potato, scrubbed	1 medium
4oz	short noodles	125g
1 clove	garlic	1 clove
½oz	pine nuts or flaked almonds	15g
2oz	ricotta or skimmed milk soft cheese	50g
½ teaspoon	dried basil	1 x 2.5ml spoon
2 teaspoons	olive oil	1 x 10ml spoon

1 Boil potato until tender. Drain, slice and return to pan.

2 Cook noodles in lightly salted boiling water until just tender. Drain and add to potato slices.

3 Pound together garlic, nuts, cheese and basil. Mix in oil.

4 Fold nut purée into potato and noodles and reheat gently. Add a little water if necessary.

Serving suggestion. Wholemeal bread and salad of sliced chicory, diced red pepper and cooked peas with Tomato and Yogurt Dressing (see page 29).

Vegetable Lasagne

SERVES 4

8 sheets	green lasagne	8 sheets
1 tablespoon	corn or sunflower oil	1 x 15ml spoon
1oz	butter or polyunsaturated margarine	25g
8oz	courgettes, topped, tailed and thinly sliced	250g
6oz	parsnips, peeled and thinly sliced	175g
6oz	red pepper, deseeded and sliced	175g
6oz	tomatoes, quartered	175g
1 clove	garlic, crushed	1 clove
½ teaspoon	dried sweet basil	1 x 2.5ml spoon
1 tablespoon	tomato purée	1 x 15ml spoon
Sauce		
4oz	mushrooms, sliced	125g
¼pt	vegetable stock	150ml
5oz	low-fat natural yogurt	150g
2	eggs	2
¼ teaspoon	ground cumin	½ x 2.5ml spoon
	ground black pepper	
1oz	Parmesan cheese, grated	25g
few sprigs	fresh basil (optional)	few sprigs

1 Pre-heat oven to 400°F/200°C/Gas Mark 6.

2 Cook lasagne in boiling salted water for 12 minutes. Drain.

3 Heat oil and butter or margarine in a large saucepan, add vegetables, garlic, basil and tomato purée. Cover and cook

gently for 20 minutes until vegetables begin to soften. Remove from heat.

4 To make sauce, cook mushrooms in stock for 8-10 minutes, cool and blend in a liquidiser or processor.

5 Make sauce up to ½pt (300ml) with yogurt, beat in eggs, cumin and black pepper.

6 Put a layer of vegetables in a 3pt (2 litre) oblong casserole, then add 2 sheets of lasagne and some sauce. Continue to add layers finishing with sauce.

7 Sprinkle with cheese and bake for 30-40 minutes until golden brown and set. Serve very hot garnished with fresh basil, if using.

Serving suggestion. Chick pea, lettuce and cucumber salad, and grapefruit and watercress salad.

Broccoli and Almond Soufflé Pudding

SERVES 4

8oz	broccoli spears	250g
½pt	skimmed or low-fat milk	300ml
2oz	fresh wholemeal breadcrumbs	50g
2oz	Edam or reduced-fat Cheddar cheese	50g
2 tablespoons	grated Parmesan cheese	2 x 15ml spoons
1 teaspoon	dry mustard	1 x 5ml spoon
½ teaspoon	salt	1 x 2.5ml spoon
	ground black pepper	
2oz	flaked almonds	50g
2	eggs, separated	2

1 Pre-heat oven to 375°F/190°C/Gas Mark 5.

2 Remove and chop broccoli stems. Break florets in small pieces. Boil stems for 5 minutes, add florets and cook for a further 5 minutes. Drain and purée in liquidiser or processor.

3 Heat milk. Put breadcrumbs in a large bowl and pour milk over them, allowing them to swell for 5 minutes. Mix in cheeses, mustard and seasoning, three-quarters of almonds, egg yolks and broccoli purée.

4 In a large bowl, whip egg whites until stiff and fold into the cheese mixture. Transfer to a greased 2pt (1 litre) soufflé dish. Sprinkle with remaining almonds.

5 Bake for about 30-35 minutes until risen and just set. Serve immediately.

Serving suggestion. Hot crusty bread and salad of sliced tomato, cucumber and chopped onion.

Vegetable Lasagne

POTATOES AND PUREES

Practically any vegetables may be cooked and puréed, but
do choose really fresh ones and don't overcook them.
Children often won't eat plain boiled vegetables, but enjoy purées

Stuffed Baked Potatoes

SERVES 1

1 large	floury potato	1 large
1 teaspoon	corn or sunflower oil	1 x 5ml spoon
	salt	

1 Pre-heat oven to 400°F/200°C/Gas Mark 6.

2 Scrub potato and score a cross on flat part.

3 Wash hands, pour oil into palms and rub all over potato skin.

4 Rub a very small amount of salt on potato.

5 Bake for 1-1½ hours until cooked through.

6 Cut potato along score lines and ease back skin. Scoop out potato flesh, mix with any of the fillings below, pile back in potato shell and serve.

Fillings

Soft cheese and ham. Mash potato with 2oz (50g) low-fat soft cheese, then stir in 1oz (25g) lean ham cut in thin strips.
Fish and corn. Flake 2oz (50g) any cooked fish, mix with 2 tablespoons (15ml spoons) cooked sweetcorn and 1 tablespoon (15ml spoon) chopped spring onion.
Curried mushroom. Cook 1oz (25g) sliced mushrooms in a knob of butter. Add 1 teaspoon (5ml spoon) mild curry powder, 1 tablespoon (15ml spoon) chopped spring onion. Use 1oz (25g) grated Edam cheese for topping.

Lemon Dill Potatoes

SERVES 4

1½lb	new potatoes, washed	750g
5oz	low-fat natural yogurt	150g
1 tablespoon	lemon juice	1 x 15ml spoon
½ teaspoon	dried dill weed	1 x 2.5ml spoon
1 tablespoon	chopped fresh parsley	1 x 15ml spoon
	ground black pepper	

1 Cook potatoes in boiling salted water for 15-20 minutes. Drain, keep warm.

2 Mix remaining ingredients in a small bowl and pour over hot potatoes. Toss and serve immediately.

Layered Potato Bake

SERVES 4

2lb	potatoes, scrubbed	1kg
5oz	low-fat natural yogurt	150g
¼pt	skimmed or low-fat milk	150ml
2 tablespoons	chopped fresh chives	2 x 15ml spoons
	ground black pepper	
2 tablespoons	grated Parmesan cheese	2 x 15ml spoons

1 Pre-heat oven to 350°F/180°C/Gas Mark 4.

2 Cut potatoes in ½ inch (1.5cm) slices and cook in boiling salted water for 5 minutes, drain.

3 Mix together yogurt, milk, chives and pepper. Put a layer of potatoes on base of an oiled ovenproof dish, cover with a layer of yogurt mixture and continue adding layers until dish is full ending with yogurt mixture.

4 Sprinkle with Parmesan cheese and bake for 45-50 minutes until crisp and golden brown.

Brussels Sprout and Nut Purée

SERVES 4

1lb	Brussels sprouts, trimmed and washed	500g
3 tablespoons	single or soured cream	3 x 15ml spoons
¼ teaspoon	salt	½ x 2.5ml spoon
	ground black pepper	
¼ teaspoon	ground nutmeg	½ x 2.5ml spoon
2oz	flaked almonds or pinenuts, toasted	50g

1 Boil Brussels sprouts in very little water, or steam until just tender. Do not overcook. Drain well.

2 Transfer to a liquidiser or processor, add cream, salt, pepper and nutmeg. Blend until smooth.

3 Stir in nuts and serve hot.

Carrot and Lentil Purée

SERVES 4

Carrots must be cooked until they are soft so they can be puréed easily.

4oz	lentils	125g
¾pt	vegetable stock	450ml
1lb	carrots, washed and sliced	500g
1 clove	garlic, crushed	1 clove
1 teaspoon	lemon juice	1 x 5ml spoon
¼ teaspoon	ground nutmeg	½ x 2.5ml spoon
	ground black pepper	
½oz	butter or polyunsaturated margarine	15g
1-2 tablespoons	skimmed or low-fat milk	1-2 x 15ml spoons
1 tablespoon	chopped fresh parsley	1 x 15ml spoon

1 Put lentils and stock in a saucepan, boil, skim, then cover pan and simmer gently for 20 minutes until liquid is absorbed. Cool.

2 Cook carrots in boiling salted water until soft. Drain and cool.

3 Put lentils, carrots, garlic, lemon juice, nutmeg and pepper in a liquidiser or processor and blend until smooth.

4 Heat butter or margarine and milk in a saucepan, add purée and reheat gently. Serve garnished with chopped parsley.

Stuffed Baked Potato with Curried Mushroom filling

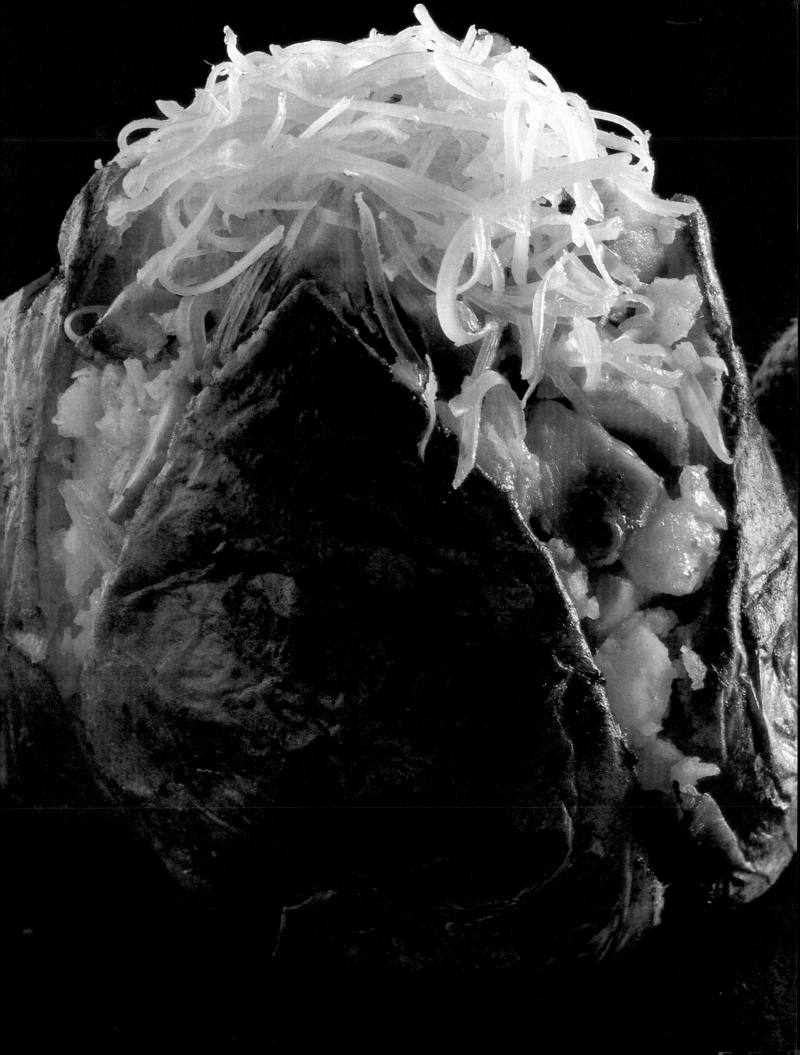

STIR-FRIES

Stir-fries are much more interesting than
plain boiled vegetables

Stir-Fry Winter Medley

SERVES 4

1lb	small Brussels sprouts, trimmed and washed	500g
2 tablespoons	corn or sunflower oil	2 x 15ml spoons
1	onion, sliced	1
3	carrots, washed and cut in sticks	3
2 cloves	garlic, crushed	2 cloves
2 teaspoons	clear honey	1 x 10ml spoon
2 tablespoons	light soy sauce	2 x 15ml spoons
1 tablespoon	dry sherry	1 x 15ml spoon
2 teaspoons	cornflour	1 x 10ml spoon
2oz	unsalted cashew nuts	50g

1 Cut sprouts in half lengthways. Heat oil in a large frying pan and
fry all vegetables and garlic together, stirring continuously for
about 5 minutes until lightly cooked but still crisp.

2 Mix honey, soy sauce, sherry and cornflour and add to
vegetables. Stir until thickened. Sprinkle in cashews.

Sweet and Sour Stir-Fry

SERVES 4

1 tablespoon	corn or sunflower oil	1 x 15ml spoon
1 teaspoon	fresh ginger, finely chopped	1 x 5ml spoon
1 teaspoon	fresh green chilli, deseeded and finely chopped	1 x 5ml spoon
4 large	spring onions, finely sliced	4 large
1lb	mangetout, trimmed	500g
2 tablespoons	white wine vinegar	2 x 15ml spoons
2 tablespoons	light soy sauce	2 x 15ml spoons
2 tablespoons	water	2 x 15ml spoons
2 teaspoons	sugar	1 x 10ml spoon
10oz can	water chestnuts, drained and sliced	280g can

1 Heat oil in a wok or large frying pan until hot. Add ginger, chilli
and spring onions and stir-fry for 1 minute.

2 Add mangetout, stir-fry for 3-4 minutes then add vinegar, soy
sauce, water and sugar. Stir-fry for a further 2 minutes. Add
water chestnuts and heat through.

Stir-Fry Summer Medley

SERVES 4

2 tablespoons	corn or sunflower oil	2 x 15ml spoons
3	spring onions, chopped	3
1 inch cube	fresh ginger, peeled and grated (optional)	1 x 2.5cm cube
2 cloves	garlic, crushed	2 cloves
4oz	mangetout, trimmed	125g
4oz	whole green beans, topped, tailed and halved	125g
4oz	broccoli florets	125g
1	red or green pepper, deseeded and thinly sliced	1
4oz	cauliflower florets	125g
4oz	white cabbage, thinly sliced	125g
2 tablespoons	light soy sauce	2 x 15ml spoons
2 tablespoons	dry cider or wine	2 x 15ml spoons
2 teaspoons	cornflour	1 x 10ml spoon
1 teaspoon	sesame oil (optional)	1 x 5ml spoon

1 Heat oil in wok or heavy-based frying pan. Add spring onions,
ginger, if using, and garlic. Stir continuously for about 1
minute.

2 Tip in all vegetables and stir continuously for about 4 minutes
until they are hot and just cooked.

3 Mix soy sauce, cider or wine and cornflour then pour over
vegetables and toss until well coated. Add sesame oil, if using,
and toss again. (Sesame oil gives a delicious flavour and is best
added at end of cooking.)

Cucumber Carrot Stir-Fry

SERVES 4

½	cucumber	½
2 large	carrots, washed	2 large
1 tablespoon	corn or sunflower oil	1 x 15ml spoon
1lb	Chinese leaves or white cabbage, thickly sliced	500g
1 clove	garlic, crushed	1 clove
1 teaspoon	fresh root ginger, chopped	1 x 5ml spoon
1 tablespoon	soy sauce	1 x 15ml spoon
1 tablespoon	dry sherry	1 x 15ml spoon

1 Cut cucumber in half lengthways, scoop out seeds with a teaspoon. Cut cucumber and carrots in 2 inch (5cm) matchsticks.

2 Heat oil in a wok or large frying pan. When hot add cucumber, carrot, Chinese leaves or cabbage, garlic and ginger, stir-fry for 3-4 minutes.

3 Add soy sauce and sherry. Fry for a further 3 minutes. Serve immediately.

Stir-Fry Winter Medley

STUFFED VEGETABLES

Filling vegetables makes them much more interesting. It's a good way to use left-overs too

Baked Stuffed Tomatoes

SERVES 4

4	jumbo ('beef') tomatoes	4
2oz	long grain rice, preferably brown	50g
½ teaspoon	turmeric	1 x 2.5ml spoon
1 tablespoon	corn or sunflower oil	1 x 15ml spoon
2 tablespoons	onion, finely chopped	2 x 15ml spoons
2oz	mushrooms, chopped	50g
2oz	almonds or unsalted peanuts, chopped and toasted	50g
1 tablespoon	chopped fresh mint	1 x 15ml spoon
1 tablespoon	chopped fresh parsley	1 x 15ml spoon
1 tablespoon	Worcestershire sauce	1 x 15ml spoon
	ground black pepper	
2 tablespoons	low-fat natural yogurt	2 x 15ml spoons

1 Pre-heat oven to 375°F/190°C/Gas Mark 5.

2 Stand each tomato on round end and remove slice from stalk end. Reserve tomato 'caps'. Scoop out seeds and discard.

3 Cook rice in boiling salted water, adding turmeric to colour, drain and rinse. Heat oil in small pan, add onion and mushrooms and cook gently until soft.

4 Combine all ingredients except tomatoes in a large bowl and use to fill tomato shells. Replace caps. Put in an ovenproof dish and bake for 15-20 minutes. Serve hot or cold.

Savoury Stuffed Cabbage Leaves

SERVES 4

½oz	butter	15g
1 small	onion, chopped	1 small
1 clove	garlic, crushed	1 clove
2oz	mushrooms, chopped	50g
6oz	cooked long grain rice, preferably brown	175g
2oz	sultanas	50g
1oz	walnuts, roughly chopped	25g
½ teaspoon	dried thyme	1 x 2.5ml spoon
	ground black pepper	
8	large Savoy cabbage leaves, hard stalks removed	8
14oz can	tomatoes	400g can
¼pt	chicken stock	150ml

1 Pre-heat oven to 400°/200°C/Gas Mark 6.

2 Melt butter in a small saucepan, add onion, garlic and mushrooms and fry gently until soft.

3 Transfer to a large bowl and add rice, sultanas, walnuts, thyme and pepper. Boil cabbage leaves for ½ minute. Drain.

4 Put 1 heaped tablespoon (15ml spoon) of stuffing on inside of each leaf at the stalk end, fold up stalk end of cabbage leaf, then fold over sides and roll up to form a parcel.

5 Mix tomatoes and stock and pour into a large ovenproof dish. Add cabbage parcels, join sides down, cover with lid or foil and bake for 40-50 minutes.

Stuffed Courgette and Pepper Bake

SERVES 4

2 large	courgettes, topped and tailed	2 large
1 tablespoon	corn or sunflower oil	1 x 15ml spoon
½ small	green pepper, deseeded and sliced	½ small
½ small	red pepper, deseeded and sliced	½ small
1 small	onion, sliced	1 small
1 clove	garlic, crushed	1 clove
2oz	flaked almonds, toasted	50g
½ teaspoon	dried thyme	1 x 2.5ml spoon
	ground black pepper	
4oz	low-fat cottage cheese	125g

1 Pre-heat oven to 400°F/200°C/Gas Mark 6.

2 Boil courgettes in salted water for 5-7 minutes, drain and cool.

3 Heat oil in a small saucepan, add peppers, onion and garlic, cover and cook slowly for 8 minutes until softened.

4 Cut courgettes in half lengthways, scoop out flesh with a teaspoon, roughly chop and add to pepper mixture, cook for a further 5 minutes. Add almonds, thyme and black pepper.

5 Fill courgettes with pepper mixture, top with cheese and put in a baking dish. Bake for 25-30 minutes until golden brown.

Greek Stuffed Aubergines

SERVES 4

2 medium	aubergines	2 medium
1 tablespoon	corn or sunflower oil	1 x 15ml spoon
2 tablespoons	water	2 x 15ml spoons
1 medium	onion, chopped	1 medium
1 clove	garlic, crushed	1 clove
1 teaspoon	ground cumin or curry powder	1 x 5ml spoon
6oz	cooked meat or fish	175g
4oz	cooked rice, preferably brown	125g
1	egg, beaten	1
1 tablespoon	chopped fresh parsley	1 x 15ml spoon
½ teaspoon	salt	1 x 2.5ml spoon
	ground black pepper	
1oz	flaked almonds	25g
2oz	white Cheshire cheese, grated	50g

1 Pre-heat oven to 350°F/180°C/Gas Mark 4.

2 Halve aubergines lengthways, scoop out flesh leaving shells intact. Blanch or steam shells for 2 minutes, drain.

3 Chop aubergine flesh and cook with oil, water, onion and garlic for 5 minutes.

4 Add cumin or curry powder and cook a further 1 minute.

5 Mix in meat or fish, rice, egg, parsley and seasoning and pile in aubergine shells. Put on a non-stick or greased baking tray, cover with foil and bake for 30 minutes.

6 Remove foil, sprinkle with almonds and cheese and cook a further 15 minutes.

Greek Stuffed Aubergines; Baked Stuffed Tomatoes

VEGETABLES WITH SAUCES

Adding tiny amounts of well-flavoured ingredients makes an enormous difference to plain boiled vegetables. Try to include at least two different vegetables, as well as potatoes, with each main meal

Courgettes Provencal

SERVES 4

1lb	courgettes, topped, tailed and sliced	500g
1 medium	onion, sliced	1 medium
2 cloves	garlic, crushed	2 cloves
4	tomatoes, sliced	4
½pt	chicken stock	300ml
	ground black pepper	
	fresh basil	

1 Pre-heat oven to 400°F/200°C/Gas Mark 6.

2 Put courgettes in an ovenproof casserole.

3 Cover with remaining ingredients. Cover casserole tightly with a lid or foil and bake for 40-50 minutes until vegetables are tender. Garnish with fresh basil.

Carrots with Thyme and Honey

SERVES 4

1lb	carrots, washed and cut in matchsticks	500g
¼pt	water	150ml
small knob	butter	small knob
1 teaspoon	honey	1 x 5ml spoon
pinch	salt	pinch
	ground black pepper	
1 tablespoon	chopped fresh parsley	1 x 15ml spoon
1 teaspoon	dried thyme	1 x 5ml spoon
	or	
3 sprigs	fresh thyme	3 sprigs

1 Put carrots in a heavy-based saucepan with water, butter, honey, salt and pepper.

2 Bring to boil, cover and simmer for about 5 minutes until just tender. Do not overcook.

3 Uncover, add parsley and thyme and cook gently until liquid has evaporated. Serve hot.

Cabbage with Lemon Caraway Dressing

SERVES 4

1lb	white or green cabbage, shredded	500g
½oz	butter or polyunsaturated margarine	15g
1 tablespoon	caraway seeds	1 x 15ml spoon
1	lemon, juice only	1
	ground black pepper	

1 Boil cabbage in very little water, or steam until just tender. Drain well.

2 Heat butter or margarine and caraway seeds in a small pan, add lemon juice and pepper.

3 Pour over cabbage and toss well to coat. Serve immediately.

Peas with Lettuce

SERVES 4

1 small	round lettuce	1 small
4	spring onions, chopped	4
¼pt	stock or water	150ml
2 tablespoons	dry cider (optional)	2 x 15ml spoons
pinch	salt	pinch
	ground black pepper	
pinch	sugar	pinch
1lb	frozen peas	500g
1 tablespoon	chopped fresh mint	1 x 15ml spoon
2 tablespoons	single cream	2 x 15ml spoons

1 Slice lettuce and put in a saucepan with spring onions, stock or water, cider, if used, seasoning and sugar. Cover and simmer for about 5 minutes.

2 Add peas and mint and simmer for a further 3-5 minutes.

3 Just before serving, remove from heat and stir in cream.

Braised Celery and Tomato

SERVES 4

Delicious as an accompaniment to meats or, with added haricot or butter beans and grated cheese, an appetising light meal.

1 head	celery, washed and sliced	1 head
1	onion, sliced	1
½oz	butter or polyunsaturated margarine	15g
¼pt	stock or water	150ml
¼ teaspoon	salt	½ x 2.5ml spoon
	(if unsalted stock or water used)	
	ground black pepper	
1 tablespoon	chopped fresh marjoram	1 x 15ml spoon
	or	
1 teaspoon	dried marjoram	1 x 5ml spoon
6	tomatoes, skinned and deseeded	6

1 Put celery, onion, butter or margarine, stock or water, seasoning and marjoram in a saucepan. Cover, bring to boil then simmer for 10 minutes.

2 Chop tomato flesh, add to saucepan, cover and simmer for a further 20 minutes. Celery should still have some 'bite'. Do not drain.

Creamed Spinach

SERVES 4

Orange and nutmeg make plain spinach something special.

2lb	fresh spinach, washed	1kg
	or	
1lb	frozen leaf spinach	500g
3 tablespoons	low-fat natural yogurt	3 x 15ml spoons
1 clove	garlic, crushed	1 clove
1	orange, grated rind and juice	1
	ground black pepper	
pinch	grated nutmeg	pinch

1 Put spinach in a large pan without any extra water, cover and cook until tender — 5-8 minutes for fresh, less for frozen.

2 Drain well, pressing in a colander to remove moisture. Sieve or blend in a liquidiser or processor.

3 Put in a large bowl and beat in yogurt, garlic, orange juice and pepper.

4 Transfer to a shallow oval serving dish and garnish with orange rind and nutmeg. Serve immediately.

Sauté Turnips in Orange

SERVES 4

1lb	turnips, peeled and cubed	500g
1oz	polyunsaturated margarine	25g
1 large	orange, grated rind and juice	1 large
	ground black pepper	
pinch	grated nutmeg	pinch

1 Sauté turnips in margarine for 3-4 minutes until just beginning to colour.

2 Add orange juice, pepper and nutmeg, simmer gently, stirring occasionally for 8-10 minutes.

3 Serve sprinkled with orange rind.

Broccoli Cauliflower Bake

SERVES 4

8oz	broccoli, washed and trimmed	250g
8oz	cauliflower florets, trimmed	250g
3 rashers	back bacon, fat removed	3 rashers
½pt	skimmed or low-fat milk	300ml
1 tablespoon	cornflour	1 x 15ml spoon
1½oz	Parmesan cheese, grated	40g
1 teaspoon	made English mustard	1 x 5ml spoon
	ground black pepper	
2oz	fresh wholemeal breadcrumbs	50g

1 Pre-heat oven to 375°F/190°C/Gas Mark 5.

2 Cook broccoli and cauliflower in boiling salted water for 8 minutes, drain and put in an ovenproof dish.

3 Grill bacon rashers on both sides, slice and put on top of vegetables.

4 Blend milk with cornflour in a saucepan, stir over a low heat until thick. Add cheese, mustard and pepper, remove from heat and stir until cheese has melted.

5 Pour sauce over vegetables, sprinkle with breadcrumbs and bake for 15-20 minutes until golden and bubbling.

Courgettes Provencal; Carrots with Thyme and Honey

JELLIES AND OMELETS

Home-made jellies may be made with practically any combination of fruits available. Sweet omelets are delicious after a light main course

Knickerbocker Jelly

SERVES 6

1 large	mango, skinned	1 large
2 small	oranges	2 small
25fl oz bottle	apple juice	70cl bottle
1	ripe banana, peeled	1
8oz	strawberries, hulled	250g
¼pt	very hot water	150ml
¾oz (2 sachets)	powdered gelatine	20g (2 sachets)

1 Cut mango flesh from stone.

2 Cut and discard orange peel and pith.

3 Put mango and orange in a liquidiser or processor, blend and transfer to a bowl.

4 Clean liquidiser. Purée 16fl oz (500ml) apple juice with banana and put in a second bowl.

5 Clean liquidiser. Put strawberries in a measuring jug, add apple juice to make up to 16fl oz (500ml). Transfer to liquidiser or processor and purée. Transfer to a third bowl or jug.

6 Pour water in a cup, sprinkle on gelatine, stir to dissolve.

7 Stir 2 tablespoons (15ml spoons) dissolved gelatine into mango mixture.

8 Divide remaining gelatine between other two purées, mix well.

9 Lightly oil a 3pt (1.5 litre) mould and pour in mango purée. Chill in refrigerator or freezer until firm.

10 Pour in banana purée, allow to set. Add strawberry purée, allow to set.

11 Demould by putting mould in hot water for a few seconds, invert on a serving plate and serve.

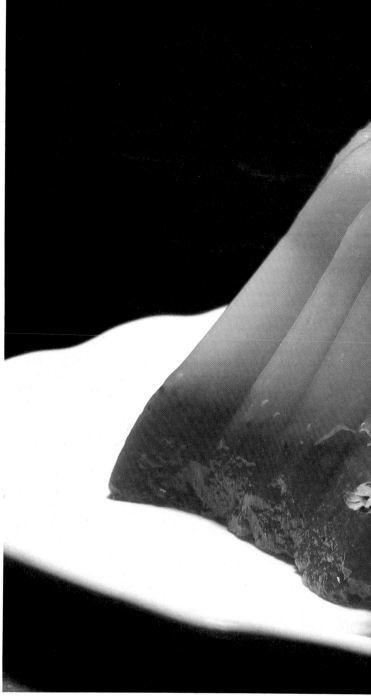

Yogurt Orange Jelly

SERVES 6

½oz	powered gelatine	15g
3 tablespoons	very hot water	3 x 15ml spoons
2 x 10½oz cans	mandarin oranges in natural juice	2 x 300g cans
1 large	orange, squeezed	1 large
5oz	low-fat orange yogurt	150g

1 Sprinkle gelatine on water in a small bowl, stir until dissolved.

2 Drain juice from mandarin oranges, make up to ½pt (300ml) with orange juice and water if necessary.

3 Put liquid in a large bowl and whisk in yogurt. Reserve a few mandarin orange segments, add remainder to juice. Stir in dissolved gelatine.

4 Pour in a 1½pt (900ml) jelly mould and leave to set. To serve, unmould and decorate with reserved mandarin orange segments.

Coffee Milk Jelly

SERVES 4

4 tablespoons	very hot water	4 x 15ml spoons
4 teaspoons	powdered gelatine	2 x 10ml spoons
1pt	skimmed or low-fat milk	600ml
2 tablespoons	soft brown sugar	2 x 15ml spoons
1 tablespoon	instant coffee powder or granules	1 x 15ml spoon
1	orange, grated rind only	1
tiny pinch	cardamom seeds (optional)	tiny pinch

1 Put hot water in a cup and sprinkle in gelatine. Stir briskly until dissolved.

2 Heat half milk with sugar and coffee, stirring until dissolved. Remove from heat, add remaining milk, orange rind and cardamom seeds, if using.

3 Add gelatine and stir well, then pour in a very lightly oiled 1pt (600ml) jelly mould. Leave in refrigerator to set.

4 Demould by first easing jelly away from sides of mould, then dip in very hot water for a few seconds and invert on a serving plate.

Fruit Soufflé Omelet

	SERVES 2	
3	eggs, separated	3
1 tablespoon	caster sugar	1 x 15ml spoon
1 tablespoon	any liqueur (optional)	1 x 15ml spoon
¼pt	any fruit filling	150ml

1 Whisk eggs with a hand or electric whisk until thick.

2 Add sugar and liqueur, if using.

3 Brush a non-stick omelet pan or small frying pan with a little oil and heat.

4 Pour in egg mixture and cook, without stirring, until underside is brown and top is just set.

5 Spoon in chosen filling, fold in half . Serve immediately.

Fruit filling suggestions

Sliced strawberries
Sliced ripe banana
Stewed apple and blackberries
Sliced mango
Warmed raspberries
Stewed gooseberries and redcurrants

Knickerbocker Jelly

MAINLY FRUIT

Advice about healthy eating frequently suggests you should eat fresh fruit instead of high-fat puddings

Fruit Medley

SERVES 4

1 large	pineapple	1 large
2 large	oranges	2 large
1	lemon	1
1	banana, peeled and sliced	1
1	kiwi fruit, peeled and sliced	1
2oz	black grapes, halved and deseeded	50g
1	fresh peach, peeled, stoned and sliced	1
3oz	fresh strawberries or raspberries, hulled	75g
2 tablespoons	orange-flavoured liqueur	2 x 15ml spoons

1 Cut top off pineapple, and keep on one side. Remove a thin slice from base so that pineapple stands safely on a large flat plate.

2 Use a sharp knife to cut out centre flesh of pineapple leaving a ½ inch (1.5cm) thick shell. Remove core and cut pineapple in chunks.

3 Peel 1 orange and cut in segments. Squeeze other orange and the lemon.

4 Mix all fruits in a large bowl and add orange juice, lemon juice and liqueur.

5 Fill pineapple shell with fruit and juice, arrange any surplus around base. Replace pineapple top and chill for at least an hour before serving.

Very Special Strawberries

SERVES 4

1lb	strawberries, washed and hulled	500g
2	passion fruits	2
8oz	raspberries, washed and hulled	250g
2 tablespoons	honey	2 x 15ml spoons
1 tablespoon	brandy, rum or kirsch (optional)	1 x 15ml spoon
	mint leaves	

1 Put strawberries, halved if large, in a mixing bowl.

2 Cut passion fruits in half, scoop seeds and flesh into a liquidiser or processor. Add raspberries, honey and alcohol, if using. Blend.

3 Pour over strawberries, mix well and chill.

4 Serve in a large dish or 4 small glass bowls. Decorate with mint.

Pineapple Banana Crunch

SERVES 4

14oz can	pineapple rings in natural juice	400g can
2	well ripened bananas, peeled	2
2oz	stoned dates, chopped	50g
2oz	wholemeal flour	50g
2oz	plain white flour	50g
1½oz	polyunsaturated margarine	40g
1oz	porridge oats	25g
1oz	desiccated coconut	25g

1 Pre-heat oven to 375°F/190°C/Gas Mark 5.

2 Drain pineapple, reserve juice and cut rings in pieces.

3 Slice bananas and add to pineapple. Put in medium-sized ovenproof dish.

4 Add chopped dates and ¼pt (150ml) pineapple juice.

5 Mix flours and work in margarine with a fork. Stir in oats and coconut.

6 Sprinkle topping over fruit and bake for about 30-35 minutes until browned.

Gooseberry Pudding

SERVES 6

6oz	dried apricots	175g
4oz	sultanas	125g
¾pt	cold water	450ml
12oz	gooseberries, trimmed	350g
8 thin slices	wholemeal bread	8 thin slices
¼pt	orange juice	150ml
2 tablespoons	clear honey	2 x 15ml spoons

1 Put apricots, sultanas and water in a saucepan, cover and simmer for 40 minutes.

2 Add gooseberries and cook for a further 15 minutes.

3 Remove crusts from bread, cut 6 slices in fingers and use to line a 1½pt (900ml) pudding basin. Sprinkle orange juice over bread.

4 Stir honey in fruit mixture and pour in basin. Put remaining 2 pieces of bread, cut to fit, on top.

5 Cover with a plate and stand a jar of jam or marmalade on top. Refrigerate for at least 8 hours before serving.

6 To serve, remove plate, invert basin on a serving plate and unmould pudding. Serve with low-fat natural yogurt or a mixture of single cream and yogurt.

Fruit Kebabs

SERVES 4

3	bananas, peeled and cut in 1 inch (2.5cm) pieces	3
8oz	pineapple chunks, fresh or canned	250g
3	peaches, peeled, stoned and cut in chunks	3
3	dessert apples, cored and cut in chunks	3
2 tablespoons	lemon juice	2 x 15ml spoons
1	orange, grated rind and juice	1
2 tablespoons	clear honey	2 x 15ml spoons
	mixed spice	

1 Put fruits in a large bowl with lemon juice and orange juice. Toss to coat all surfaces to prevent browning.

2 Thread fruits on 4 kebab skewers or wood satay sticks, brush with honey and grill. Cook for 8-10 minutes turning frequently until just beginning to colour slightly.

3 Dust with mixed spice and sprinkle with orange rind.

Fruit Kebabs

MAINLY FRUIT

Blackberry Apple Crumble

SERVES 4

This topping is much lower in fat than traditional crumble — tastier too.

8oz	blackberries, washed and hulled	250g
8oz	pears, peeled, cored and sliced	250g
8oz	cooking apples, preferably Bramley, peeled, cored and sliced	250g
½	lemon, grated rind and juice	½
2 teaspoons	caster sugar	1 x 10ml spoon
4oz	unsweetened muesli	125g
1oz	Bran Flakes, lightly crushed	25g
½ teaspoon	cinnamon	1 x 2.5ml spoon
1oz	demerara sugar	25g

1 Pre-heat oven to 375°F/190°C/Gas Mark 5.

2 Put fruits in a saucepan with lemon juice, rind and caster sugar, simmer gently for 8-10 minutes until fruit is beginning to soften. Pour in an ovenproof dish.

3 Combine muesli, Bran Flakes, cinnamon and demerara sugar, sprinkle over fruit.

4 Bake for 15-20 minutes until topping is crisp and golden brown.

Freezing note. Freeze fruit without crumble topping. To use, thaw, add topping and complete recipe as above.

Danish Apple Pudding

SERVES 4

1½lb	cooking apples, cored	750g
3 tablespoons	water	3 x 15ml spoons
1 tablespoon	honey	1 x 15ml spoon
½oz	butter or polyunsaturated margarine	15g
3oz	fresh wholemeal breadcrumbs	75g
1oz	walnuts or almonds, chopped	25g
1 tablespoon	demerara sugar	1 x 15ml spoon

1 Chop unpeeled apple and cook with water and honey until soft. Blend to a purée.

2 Melt butter or margarine and mix with breadcrumbs. This is best done with clean hands. Stir in nuts.

3 Put crumbs on a baking sheet and grill gently to brown. Stir mixture frequently to prevent burning. Stir in sugar and cool.

4 Layer purée and crumbs in glass dishes and chill well.

Cocoa Rice with Pears

SERVES 4

3	hard pears, peeled, cored and sliced	3
2oz	pudding rice	50g
1 tablespoon	cocoa powder	1 x 15ml spoon
1pt	skimmed or low-fat milk	600ml
½ teaspoon	vanilla essence	1 x 2.5ml spoon
1-2 tablespoons	soft brown sugar	1-2 x 15ml spoons

1 Pre-heat oven to 300°F/150°C/Gas Mark 2.

2 Put pears in a 1pt (600ml) pie dish. Sprinkle on rice.

3 Blend cocoa with a little cold milk until smooth. Heat remaining milk with essence and sugar.

4 Pour hot milk on cocoa, mix and pour back in saucepan. Stirring, bring to boil, then pour on pears and rice. Mix well.

5 Bake for about 2 hours, stirring gently twice during first hour to make creamy. Serve hot or cold.

Strawberry and Kiwi Fruit Cream

SERVES 4

Use any combination of soft fruits for this mouthwatering summer sweet.

8oz	strawberries, hulled	250g
2	kiwi fruit, skinned	2
5oz	low-fat or skimmed milk soft cheese	150g
5oz	low-fat peach melba yogurt	150g
2 tablespoons	single cream	2 x 15ml spoons
1oz	flaked almonds, toasted	25g

1 Slice strawberries and kiwi fruit. Arrange on base of a large glass bowl or 4 small bowls.

2 In a large bowl break up cheese with a fork. Beat in yogurt and cream, pour over fruit.

3 Decorate with almonds and chill well.

Semolina Apple Pudding

SERVES 4

1lb	cooking apples, preferably Bramley, peeled, cored and sliced	500g
1 tablespoon	lemon juice	1 x 15ml spoon
1	orange, grated rind and juice	1
2oz	sultanas	50g
8	glacé cherries, quartered	8
1pt	skimmed or low-fat milk	600ml
2oz	semolina	50g
1oz	soft brown sugar	25g
1oz	flaked almonds, toasted	25g

1 Put apples in a saucepan with lemon juice, orange juice, sultanas and cherries. Cover and simmer gently for 10-15 minutes until apple is soft.

2 Meanwhile put milk in another saucepan, sprinkle on semolina, sugar and orange rind. Heat gently, stirring continuously, until semolina has boiled and thickened. Cook for 2 minutes, stirring.

3 Spread fruit mixture in a deep dish and pour semolina on top. Decorate with flaked almonds. Serve hot or cold.

Blackberry Apple Crumble

MOUSSES AND SORBETS

You don't need an ice cream machine to make delicious sorbets.
If they have been in the freezer for a day or two, do allow them to soften slightly
in the fridge before serving

Fruity Yogurt Mousse

SERVES 4

½oz	powdered gelatine	15g
3 tablespoons	very hot water	3 x 15ml spoons
5oz	low-fat natural or fruit yogurt	150g
¼pt	orange juice	150ml
1½oz	nibbed almonds, toasted	40g
2	egg whites	2
2 tablespoons	single cream	2 x 15ml spoons
1	orange, peeled and sliced	1

1 Sprinkle gelatine on water in a small basin, stir to dissolve.

2 Whisk yogurt and orange juice, stir in dissolved gelatine and 1oz (25g) of almonds.

3 Whisk egg whites until stiff but not dry and fold carefully into yogurt mixture. Add cream as mixture is beginning to set.

4 Spoon in individual serving dishes. Chill until set and decorate with slices of fresh orange and remaining almonds.

Freezing note. Freeze without decoration. To use, thaw and decorate.

Iced Raspberry Yogurt

SERVES 4

Any well-flavoured soft fruit may be used in this recipe.

8oz	fresh or frozen raspberries	250g
1 tablespoon	honey	1 x 15ml spoon
1oz	soft brown sugar	25g
1	well ripened banana, peeled	1
5oz	low-fat natural yogurt	150g
1	egg white	1
	mint leaves	

1 Purée raspberries with honey, sugar and banana.

2 Stir in yogurt and put in a shallow container. Freeze.

3 When ice crystals have formed in the outer ½ inch (1.5cm), transfer mixture to a chilled bowl, beat to a slush.

4 Whip egg white until stiff and fold into raspberry mixture. Return to shallow container and freeze.

5 Allow to stand in refrigerator for about 30 minutes before serving. Decorate with mint leaves.

Apricot and Prune Fluffies

SERVES 4

4oz	dried apricots	125g
4oz	dried prunes	125g
½pt	orange juice	300ml
½pt	apple juice	300ml
2	egg whites	2
1 tablespoon	flaked almonds	1 x 15ml spoon

1 Soak apricots and prunes overnight in orange juice and apple juice.

2 Simmer, covered, for about 30 minutes until soft. Remove and discard prune stones. Purée fruit and juices, chill well.

3 Whisk egg whites until stiff but not dry, fold into fruit purée.

4 Divide mixture between 4 individual glass dishes, sprinkle with almonds. Chill and serve within 30 minutes.

Rhubarb Banana Sorbet

SERVES 4

1lb	rhubarb, washed and sliced	500g
1oz	demerara sugar	25g
2 tablespoons	orange juice	2 x 15ml spoons
1 large	banana, peeled and mashed	1 large
2	egg whites	2

1 Put rhubarb in a saucepan, cover with cold water. As soon as it boils, drain and rinse in cold water.

2 Return rhubarb to saucepan with sugar and orange juice, cover and cook gently for 5 minutes until softened. Cool.

3 Blend banana with rhubarb in a liquidiser or processor until creamy.

4 Pour mixture in a shallow freezing container and freeze until crystals form in outer ½ inch (1.5cm).

5 Whisk egg whites until stiff but not dry. Transfer rhubarb mixture to a large bowl, break down with a fork and carefully fold in egg whites.

6 Return mixture to its container and freeze until firm.

7 Allow to stand in refrigerator for 1 hour before serving.

Apricot and Prune Fluffies; Iced Raspberry Yogurt

RECIPE INDEX AND
FAT, FIBRE AND CALORIE VALUES

All figures relate to 1 serving unless stated otherwise.

SNACKS AND STARTERS

Page		Fat g	Fibre g	Energy Calories
Soups				
18	Carrot and celery soup	2	4	55
20	Chilled avocado soup	8	1	170
20	Minestrone	4	8	180
18	Paprika and onion soup	7	4	180
18	Prawn and leek chowder	5	6	160
20	Red bean chilli soup	8	8	140
18	Spinach and potato soup	5	6	120
21	Watercress and orange soup	5	2	180
Patés and dips				
22	Avocado dip	9	2	120
22	Baked tuna paté	5	1	110
22	Rosy prawn dip	3	1	100
22	Smoked fish paté	9	2	220
22	Vegetable lentil dip	5	4	150
Salads				
26	Bean, rice and mushroom salad	4	12	270
26	Chinese leaf and beansprout salad	6	3	110
24	Pasta and salmon salad	10	5	330
24	Sunny salad	7	3	120
26	Swedish chicken salad	8	4	260
26	Turnip, date and apple salad	0	5	90
Dressings – whole recipe				
29	Creamy dill dressing	4	0	200
29	Orange yogurt dressing	0	2	130
29	Provencal dressing	30	0	300
29	Tomato and yogurt dressing	0	0	50
Toast toppings				
30	Chicken and corn grills	11	6	320
30	Devilled kidney toasts	9	4	250
30	Fluffy tuna baps	8	4	220
33	Hot liver on rye	12	5	270
33	Mushroom meringues	18	4	290
33	Pizza muffins	12	8	280
30	Prawn and mushroom toasts	8	6	230
33	Soufflé spinach mushrooms	10	8	240
30	Two-bean rarebit	7	11	250
Burgers – per burger without bread				
34	Beefy bran burgers	6	2	200
37	Chick pea and rice croquettes	9	4	160
34	Nut rissoles	15	7	200
37	Old fashioned rissoles	5	2	130
34	Pork burgers	5	1	110
37	Smoked fish burgers	1	1	55
37	Veal and sweet pepper burgers	4	2	200
Bakes				
38	Apple drop scones – 1	2	2	100
38	Carrot, banana and walnut loaf – whole loaf	138	36	3000
38	Cottage cheese medallions – 1	4	1	70
39	Garibaldi biscuits – 1	5	1	110

MAIN MEALS

Page		Fat g	Fibre g	Energy Calories
Fish				
43	Fish balls in tomato sauce	5	3	200
42	Prawn and corn pancakes	12	5	320
40	Seafood cheesecake	9	1	210
42	Smoked haddock roulade	17	1	340
40	Stuffed mackerel parcels	23	3	360
40	Trout with lemon sauce	6	6	220
Poultry				
47	Chicken and broccoli flan	18	6	350
47	Chicken and spinach terrine	5	3	160
47	Chicken lemon soufflé	12	2	240
44	Chicken pasta with lemon and tarragon	10	9	470
44	Turkey fillet with grapes and peanuts	13	2	330
44	Turkey tandoori	3	0	160
Beef				
50	Chilli beef and bean pot	11	9	300
48	Fruity beef casserole	13	8	300
50	Pasticcio	13	6	420
48	Pot roast beef	18	4	400
51	Spice and nut meat loaf	8	3	210
49	Steaks with orange stuffing	13	3	290
Pork and lamb				
53	Curried lamb with chick peas	16	13	380
52	Pork, parsnip and coconut casserole	20	8	350
52	Pork tenderloin stuffed with prunes	12	3	270
52	Portuguese style chops	14	5	260
Veal				
54	Fennel and orange veal escalopes	14	5	550
54	Veal mediterranean style	8	9	380
54	Veal stroganoff	9	1	170
Offal				
56	Kidney creole	11	3	250
57	Leek and liver sauté	13	1	240
56	Liver, pea and corn risotto	14	9	500
Mainly vegetarian				
61	Broccoli and almond soufflé pudding	13	5	240
58	Egg foo yong omelet	16	2	220
58	Lentil bolognese sauce	4	7	200
61	Pasta pesto	10	6	430
58	Spaghetti alla carbonara	18	6	480
58	Spiced vegetable bake	10	6	230
61	Vegetable lasagne	13	7	340

VEGETABLES

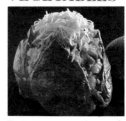

Page		Fat g	Fibre g	Energy Calories
Potatoes and purées				
62	Brussels sprout and nut purée	9	7	120

PUDDINGS

FAT, FIBRE AND CALORIE VALUES OF EVERYDAY FOODS

	Amount of food		Fat g	Fibre g	Energy Calories
All-Bran	4 tablespoons	2oz/50g	3	15	150
Apple, cooking	1 medium	9oz/250g	0	6	80
eating	1 medium	5oz/150g	0	3	60
Apricots, fresh	2	1oz/25g	0	1	10
dried	4 halves	1oz/25g	0	7	50
Avocado pear	1 small	5oz/150g	23	2	240
Bacon, streaky, cooked	1 rasher	⅓oz/10g	4	0	50
back, cooked	1 rasher	¾oz/20g	7	0	80
Banana	1 medium with skin	5oz/150g	0	3	70
Beans, baked	small can	5oz/150g	1	11	95
broad	20	1oz/25g	0	1	15
butter	20 dry weight	1oz/25g	0	6	75
red kidney	40 dry weight	1oz/25g	0	7	75
runner		1oz/25g	0	1	10
Beef, lean, stewed	2 large cubes	1oz/25g	1	0	55
lean, roast	1 small slice	1oz/25g	1	0	55
minced, cooked		1oz/25g	1-6	0	55-100
Beefburger, cooked	1 small	2oz/57g	9	0	130
Beer, lager	½pt		0	0	80
pale ale	½pt		0	0	90
stout	½pt		0	0	110
Beetroot, boiled	1 baby beet	2oz/50g	0	1	20
Biscuits, chocolate	eg 2 finger Kit Kat	¾oz/20g	6	0	110
sandwich	1	⅓oz/10g	3	0	60
digestive	1	½oz/15g	3	1	70
cream cracker	1	¼oz/8g	1	0	35
water	1 large	¼oz/8g	1	0	35
Blackberries	1 tablespoon	1oz/25g	0	2	10
Blackcurrants	1 tablespoon	1oz/25g	0	2	10
Bran	1 tablespoon	⅙oz/5g	0	2	10
Bread, white	1 medium cut slice	1oz/25g	0	1	70
long white roll	1	4oz/110g	0	4	250
wholemeal	1 medium cut slice	1oz/25g	1	2	65
pitta, white	1 piece	2½oz/70g	1	3	165
Broccoli	1 large spear	2oz/50g	0	2	10
Brussels sprouts	2	2oz/50g	0	2	10
Butter		1oz/25g	23	0	210
Cabbage		2oz/50g	0	1	10
Cake, fruit	small slice	2oz/50g	6	2	170
jam sponge	large slice	2oz/50g	3	0	150
Carrot	1 large	2oz/50g	0	1	10
Cauliflower		2oz/50g	0	1	10
Celery	large stick	2oz/50g	0	1	5
Cheese, Cheddar-type		1oz/25g	10	0	120
reduced-fat Cheddar		1oz/25g	5	0	75
cottage	small pot	4oz/113g	4	0	110
low-fat soft		1oz/25g	3	0	45
Edam		1oz/25g	7	0	90
Parmesan		1oz/25g	8	0	120
Cherries	8	2oz/50g	0	1	20
Chicken, joint, no skin	1	8oz/225g	6	0	160
roast, no skin	small slice	1oz/25g	1	0	40
Chocolate, milk	small bar	2oz/50g	15	0	300
Cider, dry	½pt		0	0	100
Coca cola	small can	7fl oz/200ml	0	0	75
Cod, baked or poached	small steak	4oz/110g	1	0	80
fried in batter	medium portion	4oz/110g	12	0	200
Corned beef	1 medium slice	1oz/25g	3	0	55
Cornflakes	6 tablespoons	¾oz/20g	0	2	75
Cream, single	1 tablespoon	½oz/15g	3	0	30
whipping	1 tablespoon	½oz/15g	5	0	50
double	1 tablespoon	½oz/15g	7	0	65
Cucumber	2 inch/5cm	3oz/75g	0	0	10
Dates	5	1oz/25g	0	2	75
Egg, raw/boiled/poached	1	2oz/55g	6	0	85
fried	1	2oz/55g	11	0	125
Egg white	1	1½oz/40g	0	0	15
Egg yolk	1	¾oz/20g	6	0	70

Amount of food		Fat g	Fibre g	Energy Calories
Fish cakes, grilled	1	2oz/50g	1	0	60
fried	1	2oz/50g	10	0	140
Fish fingers, grilled	1	1oz/25g	2	0	55
fried	1	1oz/25g	4	0	70
Flour, white	2 tablespoons	1oz/25g	0	1	100
wholemeal	2 tablespoons	1oz/25g	0	2	90
Grapefruit	1 large	10oz/300g with skin	0	1	35
Grapes	10 small	1oz/25g	0	0	15
Haddock, see cod					
Ham, lean only	1 thin slice	1oz/25g	1	0	35
Herring, grilled	1 small	7oz/200g with head	13	0	200
Honey	1 tablespoon	1oz/25g	0	0	80
Ice cream	1 small scoop	2oz/50g	4	0	90
Jam	1 tablespoon	1oz/25g	0	0	75
Kidney	1 lamb's	2oz/50g	1	0	45
Kippers	1 small fillet	2oz/50g	6	0	100
Lamb, lean only	1 small slice	1oz/25g	2	0	50
chop, lean only	1	7oz/200g with bone	12	0	210
Lard		1oz/25g	28	0	250
Leeks	1 large	3½oz/100g	0	3	30
Lentils, raw	1 tablespoon	1oz/25g	0	3	85
Lettuce	5 leaves	⅓oz/10g	0	0	1
Liqueurs	1 measure	1fl oz/25ml	0	0	75
Liver, grilled or fried	small slice	1oz/25g	3	0	60
Liver sausage		1oz/25g	7	0	90
Low-fat spread		1oz/25g	11	0	110
Mackerel	1 small	7oz/200g with head	20	0	280
Margarine		1oz/25g	23	0	210
Marmalade	1 tablespoon	1oz/25g	0	0	75
Mayonnaise	1 tablespoon	½oz/15g	12	0	110
reduced-calorie	1 tablespoon	½oz/15g	4	0	40
Meat pie, double crust	1 individual	5oz/150g	25	0	380
Melon	½ small	12oz/350g	0	2	50
Milk, whole	½pt		11	0	180
semi-skimmed	½pt		5	0	130
skimmed	½pt		0	0	95
Mushrooms, raw	3 button	2oz/50g	0	1	5
Nuts, almonds	15	1oz/25g	15	4	160
Brazil	6	1oz/25g	17	2	170
desiccated coconut	2 tablespoons	½oz/15g	9	3	90

Amount of food		Fat g	Fibre g	Energy Calories
hazelnuts	25	1oz/25g	10	2	110
peanuts	50	1oz/25g	14	2	160
walnuts	10 halves	1oz/25g	15	1	150
Oatmeal	3 tablespoons	1oz/25g	2	2	110
Oils	1 tablespoon	½oz/15g	15	0	130
Olives	6	1oz/25g with stones	2	1	25
Onions	1 medium	5oz/150g	0	2	30
Orange	1	7oz/200g with skin	0	3	50
Parsnip	1	4oz/110g	0	4	50
Pasta, dry, white		1oz/25g	0	1	100
dry, wholemeal		1oz/25g	0	3	90
Peach	1	4oz/110g	0	1	40
Pear	1	5oz/150g	0	2	45
Peas	1 tablespoon	1oz/25g	0	2	25
Pineapple	1 slice	2oz/50g	0	1	30
Pizza	1 medium	8oz/225g	28	2	630
Pork, lean only, roast	small slice	1oz/25g	2	0	55
chop, lean only	1	6oz/175g with bone	11	0	230
Potato, boiled/baked	1 medium	8oz/225g	0	5	180
roast	1 medium	5oz/150g	7	5	235
chips	20	4oz/110g	14	5	310
crisps	small pkt	1oz/25g	9	3	135
Prawns	5 small	1oz/25g	0	0	25
Prunes	4	1oz/25g	0	4	40
Raisins	1 tablespoon	1oz/25g	0	2	70
Raspberries	12	1oz/25g	0	2	10
Rice, raw, white		1oz/25g	0	1	100
raw, brown		1oz/25g	0	1	100
Salmon		1oz/25g	3	0	50
Sardine	1	1oz/25g	3	0	45
Sausage, cooked	1 large	2oz/50g	10	0	125
Semolina	1 tablespoon	1oz/25g	0	1	100
Spinach, cooked	1 tablespoon	1oz/25g	0	2	10
Spirits	single	1fl oz/25ml	0	0	60
Sugar, white/brown	1 tablespoon	1oz/25g	0	0	110
Sweetcorn	1 tablespoon	1oz/25g	0	2	25
Tomato	1	2oz/50g	0	1	10
Trout	1 small	6oz/175g	5	0	150
Veal, cooked	small slice	1oz/25g	1	0	40
Wine	small glass	4fl oz/110ml	0	0	80
Yogurt, low-fat natural	small tub	5oz/150g	1	0	80
low-fat fruit	small tub	5oz/150g	1	0	140
low-fat nut	small tub	5oz/150g	4	1	160